The Business of Bobbysoxers

The Business of Bobbysoxers

*Cultural Production in 1940s
Frank Sinatra Fandom*

KATIE BEISEL HOLLENBACH

OXFORD
UNIVERSITY PRESS

Oxford University Press is a department of the University of Oxford. It furthers the University's objective of excellence in research, scholarship, and education by publishing worldwide. Oxford is a registered trade mark of Oxford University Press in the UK and certain other countries.

Published in the United States of America by Oxford University Press
198 Madison Avenue, New York, NY 10016, United States of America.

© Oxford University Press 2024

All rights reserved. No part of this publication may be reproduced, stored in a retrieval system, or transmitted, in any form or by any means, without the prior permission in writing of Oxford University Press, or as expressly permitted by law, by license, or under terms agreed with the appropriate reproduction rights organization. Inquiries concerning reproduction outside the scope of the above should be sent to the Rights Department, Oxford University Press, at the address above.

You must not circulate this work in any other form
and you must impose this same condition on any acquirer.

Library of Congress Cataloging-in-Publication Data
Names: Hollenbach, Katie Beisel, author.
Title: The business of bobbysoxers : cultural production in 1940s Frank Sinatra fandom / Katie Beisel Hollenbach.
Description: New York : Oxford University Press, 2024. |
Includes bibliographical references and index.
Identifiers: LCCN 2024026045 (print) | LCCN 2024026046 (ebook) |
ISBN 9780197659182 (hardback) | ISBN 9780197659205 (epub)
Subjects: LCSH: Popular music—Social aspects—United States—History—20th century. |
Popular music—United States—1941-1950—History and criticism. | Sinatra, Frank, 1915-1998. |
Teenage girls—United States—History—20th century. |
Popular culture—United States—History—20th century. | Women popular music fans.
Classification: LCC ML3917.U6 H65 2024 (print) | LCC ML3917.U6 (ebook) |
DDC 782.421640973/09044—dc23/eng/20240719
LC record available at https://lccn.loc.gov/2024026045
LC ebook record available at https://lccn.loc.gov/2024026046

DOI: 10.1093/oso/9780197659182.001.0001

Printed by Marquis Book Printing, Canada

For my family

Contents

Acknowledgments   ix

   Introduction: Fan Perspectives   1

1. Teenage Girls in Wartime American Culture   15
2. Teenage Social Organizations   43
3. Finding "the Voice": Organized Fandom as Political Platform   73
4. Fans as Critics and Material Culture Makers   101
5. Postwar Changes: A New Sinatra and the Decline of the Bobbysoxers   129

   Conclusion: Popular Remembrance   153

Bibliography   157
Index   165

Acknowledgments

This book stemmed from a happy accident when I came across a collection of Frank Sinatra fan club newsletters in the Hoboken Historical Museum's digital archives while looking for other information related to the singer. As they say, the rest is history, and there are many people to thank along the way.

I'd like to first thank Gayle Sherwood Magee, Christina Bashford, Jeffrey Magee, and Julie Turnock, who provided much needed support and guidance during this project's origins as a dissertation at the University of Illinois. Their ideas, questions, and encouragement continue to inspire and influence how I approach all of my research.

Transforming this project into a book was the ultimate exercise in stepping back from the details to search for the bird's-eye view of this particular group and moment in history. I thank Mark Duffett for his invaluable mentorship in forming the structure and presentation of this book, not to mention his willingness to trade ideas and sources on popular music fandom. His work served as one of my earliest introductions into fan studies as a student and it is a privilege to now count him as a mentor and colleague. I also thank Lauralee Yeary and the team at Oxford University Press for their support and enthusiasm for this project.

The heart of this study lies in the artifacts created by teenage fans of Frank Sinatra and other popular culture figures in the 1940s, the majority of which are located in the collections of the Hoboken Historical Museum. In particular, I thank Randolph Hoppe for his great help in locating, preserving, and sharing these incredible materials. I also thank the Margaret Herrick Library of the Academy of Motion Picture Arts and Sciences; the Stuart A. Rose Manuscript, Archives, and Rare Book Library at Emory University; the Paley Center for Media; and the Media History Digital Library for their stewardship of popular culture history. I am also grateful for the generous support of the Nicholas Temperley Dissertation Prize, which allowed me to travel to and access many of these important institutions.

Thanks to Whitney Henderson, without whom I'd probably still be stuck writing Chapter 1. Her ideas, editing skills, shared affinity for music clubs, and friendship have played a key role in this book's development.

I send my great love and thanks to my parents, who have always supported my endeavors not only without question, but with constant sincerity, belief, and love. And finally, endless gratitude and love to Myles and Ian, who make it all worth it.

Introduction

Fan Perspectives

In 1944, Warner Bros. Pictures produced a short *Looney Tunes* film titled *Swooner Crooner*. The short stars Porky Pig as the supervisor of the World War II "Flockheed Eggcraft Factory," where chatty hens who are clearly meant to represent female war workers clock in every day to diligently lay eggs for the war effort. The hens are hard at work sitting on conveyor belt nests, when a disembodied voice begins to sing Max Steiner and Kim Gannon's song "It Can't Be Wrong." The hens suddenly stop working and run outside, crying, "It's Frankie!"

The film then moves outside of the factory, where viewers see a comically skinny rooster caricature of Frank Sinatra. The rooster is wearing one of Sinatra's signature oversized floppy bowties while serenading the hens, who are now portrayed not as devoted war workers, but as hysterical and ridiculous fans. The hens are swooning, screaming, literally melting into puddles, panting, and wearing the stereotypical item of war-era teenage Sinatra fans, bobby socks and saddle shoes. Porky Pig panics and is only able to get the hens back on their egg-laying track when he secures a performance by a more appropriately male singer, the rooster version of Bing Crosby.

Swooner Crooner is a near-perfect eight-minute representation of how Frank Sinatra and his teenage female fans were portrayed in media during World War II. Images of a physically weak and vulnerable pop idol and the shockingly hysterical behavior his fans demonstrated in response to him permeated newspapers and fueled concern from much of adult society, who accused both teenage girls and Sinatra of being inappropriately distracted and disengaged from the international crisis at hand. Viewing this film today may yield amused interest in the way 1940s Hollywood chose to portray one of the most well-known popular singers of all time, but as this book will show, viewers can also use the film to question how World War II American popular culture, girlhood, race, and sexuality was represented in the public imagination.

What images, sounds, and narratives come to mind when we think of World War II America in the twenty-first century? In particular, what kind of representations of war-era American women has popular collective memory preserved? Films, graphic art, music, works of fiction, and countless other cultural objects created in the decades since the war have established World War II as a time when American women stepped into new roles in service of their country and shifted the trajectory of women's history and opportunities. Rosie the Riveter reigns in historical memory as the ultimate symbol of working women, alongside images of women in uniform who served as nurses, WAACs (Women's Army Auxiliary Corps, later WACs), WASPs (Women Airforce Service Pilots), WAVES (Women Accepted for Volunteer Emergency Service), and SPARs (Semper Paratus—Always Ready). We also remember celebrities. Glamorous film stars such as Betty Grable and Rita Hayworth and uplifting musicians such as the Andrews Sisters and Kate Smith. Then there are those women who did not enter the workforce or perform but practiced their patriotism through volunteering, rationing supplies, tending to victory gardens, and supporting their loved ones overseas. While these dominant images work to rightfully emphasize the extremely important roles women held in the unfolding of one of the most significant conflicts in world history, they also reinforce the notion that the women heroes of World War II were white, of working age, and conventionally beautiful, even when donning boiler suits.

But what about those women who were too young to work or serve in the military? What about teenage girls? How do we remember them? Images of soda shops, sweaters, saddle shoes, swooning at the sight of Frank Sinatra, and again whiteness typically come to mind, sometimes alongside the word "bobbysoxer," a descriptive yet usually condescending term referencing typical fashion and popular culture consumption of 1940s teenage girls. Rather than remembering teenage girls as contributors, as we usually do adult American women during the war, popular memory tends to suggest that teenage girls instead enjoyed a certain level of blissful ignorance of the happenings around them, focusing their efforts not on work or the war effort, but on dancing, socializing, and entertainment in general. The historical narrative surrounding wartime teenage girls, although limited, has painted them primarily as consumers, not producers.

And what about Frank Sinatra? How does popular memory illustrate him? A brief overview here of Sinatra's early life and career will help to provide context for this examination.

Born in 1915, Sinatra lived a relatively well-off life in Hoboken, New Jersey, even through the Great Depression. His parents had immigrated from Italy and were active in the Hoboken community. His mother, Natalina "Dolly" Garaventa, worked as a midwife and was active in local Democratic Party politics. His father, Antonio Martino "Marty" Sinatra, was a professional boxer and fireman. The family later owned a tavern, where the young Sinatra occasionally sang. Growing up, Sinatra listened to and admired singers such as Gene Austin, Rudy Vallée, and Bing Crosby and hoped to pursue a career in music early on.

Sinatra's first break came when he joined a local singing group in 1935, the Three Flashes, which then became the Hoboken Four. The group auditioned for the radio talent program *Major Bowes Amateur Hour*, winning first place and a six-month touring and radio broadcast contract, with Sinatra as the lead singer. His next break came while working as a singing waiter at the Rustic Cabin, a New Jersey roadhouse affiliated with the New York radio station WNEW. This led to opportunities for Sinatra to perform on the network, and in 1939 he was heard by the famous bandleader Harry James, who offered Sinatra a two-year contract to sing with his band. Sinatra released his first commercial recording with the band that same year, though it did not initially sell well.

Sinatra was quickly dissatisfied with the progression of his career as a member of Harry James's band and left the group toward the end of 1939 to join Tommy Dorsey's. Sinatra enjoyed increasing commercial success with Dorsey into the early 1940s, convincing Dorsey to let him record some solo work in 1942. After this, Sinatra decided it was time to leave the band and go solo, which he was only able to do after a legal battle with Dorsey to dismantle their initial contract. Sinatra was ultimately released in 1942 and free to begin his solo career. Rumors suggested that Sinatra and Dorsey never reconciled after their split, but Sinatra always cited Dorsey as a major influence in his musical development.

Although Sinatra had become fairly well known by 1942, popular lore often credits his ultimate skyrocket to fame to his supporting performance for Benny Goodman at the Paramount in New York on December 30, 1942. The performance lives in popular memory as the night the theater became overrun with hysterical teenagers who were there not to see Goodman, but the "Extra Added Attraction," Frank Sinatra. Shortly after, Sinatra signed with Columbia Records in 1943 in the middle of the 1942–1944 strike of the American Federation of Musicians. This meant any new records Sinatra made would not be allowed to have instruments, which proved unsuccessful, but he still managed to catapult to fame as a prominent voice on radio and in live performances, and through the re-release of his 1939 recording of "All or Nothing at All" with Harry James. In the mid-1940s he began to enjoy additional success as a film actor.

As we will see in Chapter 5, Sinatra struggled through a career slump in the late 1940s into the early 1950s, caused by a variety of factors including a vocal injury, negative press coverage of his divorce from his first wife and affair with Ava Gardner, low record sales, and low film ratings. Sinatra made a remarkable comeback in 1953, however, with the success of his performance in *From Here to Eternity*, for which he won an Academy Award. Around the same time, Sinatra signed with Capitol Records and morphed into the celebrity he would remain through the rest of his extraordinary sixty-year career, which included multiple film successes, starting his own record label, countless successful records, and arguably defining the cultural identity of Las Vegas as a member of the Rat Pack. Though his voice began to decline in the 1980s, Sinatra maintained a devoted fan base and sang on stage for the last time in 1995 during a tribute for his eightieth birthday. He died in 1998 one of the most famous figures in popular culture history.[1]

Sinatra's celebrity image for the majority of his career was one of an often vulnerable, yet undeniably masculine saloon singer, but this was not always the case. Throughout the years of World War II, Sinatra was ridiculed by many for his scrawny appearance, sentimental musicality, absence from the military, and most prominently, the largely teenage and female fan base he cultivated. Compared to fans of more conventionally masculine stars during World War II, this feminization of Sinatra only increased the public scrutiny his young female fans experienced. But why has this period in Sinatra's career been overlooked both in popular memory and scholarship? The easy answer could be that this decade represents only a short blip in the overall length of Sinatra's career. A more thorough answer, however, which this book will work to provide, is that popular culture placed more value on Sinatra's celebrity work once he achieved an image, sound, and audience that was deemed more appropriately masculine and adult than the feminized image and young audience he maintained during World War II.

---

[1] Examples of more thorough biographies of Sinatra include James Kaplan, *Frank: The Voice* (New York: Anchor Books, 2010); Will Friedwald, *Sinatra! The Song Is You: A Singer's Art* (New York: Scribner, 1995); and Charles L. Granata, *Sessions with Sinatra: Frank Sinatra and the Art of Recording* (Chicago: A Cappella Books, 2004).

This study is ultimately one of remembrance: how history remembers certain people during certain times, and how by shifting perspectives and the historical sources we consult, completely different narratives can surface which shed new light on histories we think we already know. Specifically, this book challenges the dominant story of American teenage girls during World War II by exploring wartime popular culture fan communities, which reveal a group of citizens defined not by frivolous consumerism, but by creativity, activism, and thoughtful engagement with their peers. Examining wartime girl culture through the perspectives of girls themselves as opposed to mass media coverage or psychological assessments creates a new window on the history of American youth, popular culture, and World War II, one that reveals the voices and stories of a social group who have generally been excluded in these histories.

The study of youth and female music fan communities is not new. Influential work has been done that considers fandom through the lenses of gender, sexuality, consumerism, and youth culture, highlighting the cultural practices of fan communities surrounding stars and movements such as Rudy Vallée, Elvis Presley, the Beatles, and Riot Grrrl, among others.[2] Growing attention is also being given to current fan communities operating on larger scales, such as online and at comic cons.[3] Studies of fandom prior to the 1950s and 1960s, and particularly during the years of World War II, remain scarce, however, creating a gap and opportunity to examine popular music fandom in the context of one of the United States' most tumultuous eras. While the 1940s fan communities surrounding Frank Sinatra share certain similarities with previously studied fan communities—examples being the creation of zines in Riot Grrrl communities, the idolization of feminized and androgynous male stars like the Beatles and Justin Bieber, questions of fan anonymity and expression in online fan communities, and accusations of lowbrow tastes toward 1960s teenyboppers[4]—studying this

---

[2] Examples include Allison McCracken, *Real Men Don't Sing: Crooning in American Culture* (Durham, NC: Duke University Press, 2015); Erika Doss, *Elvis Culture: Fans, Faith & Image* (Lawrence: University Press of Kansas, 1999); Candy Leonard, *Beatleness: How the Beatles and Their Fans Remade the World* (New York: Arcade Publishing, 2014); and Joanne Gottlieb and Gayle Wald, "Smells Like Teen Spirit: Riot Grrrls, Revolution and Women in Independent Rock," in *Microphone Fiends: Youth Music & Youth Culture*, ed. Andrew Ross and Tricia Rose (New York: Routledge, 1994), 250–274.

[3] Examples include Henry Jenkins, *Fans, Bloggers, and Gamers: Exploring Participatory Culture* (New York: New York University Press, 2006); and Ben Bolling and Matthew J. Smith, eds., *It Happens at Comic-Con: Ethnographic Essays on a Pop Culture Phenomenon* (Jefferson, NC: McFarland & Co., 2014).

[4] Norma Coates, "Teenyboppers, Groupies, and Other Grotesques: Girls and Women in Rock Culture in the 1960s and early 1970s," *Journal of Popular Music Studies* 15, no. 1 (2003): 65–94.

particular fandom provides a new look into how American youth culture both influenced and was influenced by an extremely unstable time in US history: one in which understandings of national, gender, racial, class, and individual identities were thrown into disarray all at once.

Through highlighting the work of 1940s teenage Frank Sinatra fans, and specifically those who participated as members of Frank Sinatra fan clubs, this book considers new facets of reception, music criticism, and fan studies, such as, from whose perspectives do we currently remember World War II? Whom do we consider to be reputable music and cultural critics? Why should we study music history through teenage fandom? What can we gain from doing so? This book works to answer these questions by examining the societal pressures American teenage girls were facing during World War II, the distinct cultural practices of war-era Teen Canteens and Frank Sinatra fan clubs, how Sinatra's self-identity influenced the development of his fan community, how teen girls brought their fandom into the public sphere to engage with issues in civil rights and politics, and the extremely creative materials they created within their clubs, such as poetry, essays, art, and popular culture reviews.

Surrounding Conversations

Throughout the fields of fan studies, music history, and reception, women continue to hold simultaneously precarious and increasingly visible positions. Fan studies, although a relatively young field, has experienced multiple shifts in methodologies and subject emphases that view fandom through different gendered lenses. Initially, in what has been described as the first wave of fan studies, or the "Fandom Is Beautiful" phase, emphasis was placed on analyzing fans, and especially female fans, as cultural resistors and producers who use fandom as a way to challenge dominant cultural forces.[5] Later on, this early work was criticized for painting a seemingly idealized picture of fans as resistors without considering their positions as consumers in mass culture.[6] As digital fan communities have grown in recent years and

---

[5] Jonathan Gray, Cornel Sandvoss, and C. Lee Harrington, "Introduction: Why Still Study Fans?," in *Fandom*, 2nd ed.: *Identities and Communities in a Mediated World*, ed. Jonathan Gray, Cornel Sandvoss, and C. Lee Harrington (New York: New York University Press, 2017), 3.

[6] Melissa A. Click and Suzanne Scott, "Introduction," in *The Routledge Companion to Media Fandom*, ed. Melissa A. Click and Suzanne Scott (New York: Routledge, 2018), 1–2.

more and more people have been able to participate in fan activity at different levels, fan studies has shifted focus to broader notions of what it means to be a fan, distinguishing in some cases between "fans" and "followers," or those who actively participate in fan cultures versus those who enjoy certain media objects, but who "claim no larger social identity on the basis of this consumption."[7] As these various focuses in fan studies continue to evolve, some scholars have expressed concern over an apparent departure from early methodologies, and in particular, studying fan communities as feminine spaces and through feminist perspectives. Francesca Coppa, for example, encourages fan scholars to remember that while fans do make up increasingly larger communities worth studying, especially as the digital age progresses, fans are still individuals, and their participation in fan culture can reveal much about their identities and sense of personhood.[8]

As a study concerned with American girl culture and fan practices in the 1940s, it is perhaps unsurprising that this book agrees with authors such as Coppa and Suzanne Scott[9] that scholarship should not dismiss a focus on female fans, aligning in many ways with these earlier methodologies in fan studies. An emphasis is placed throughout this book, for example, on consulting material culture produced by wartime girls over professional criticism and media coverage in order to gain new insight on the lives and experiences of these overlooked World War II citizens. This exploration, however, approaches the relationship teen girl fans held with the entertainment industry in more nuanced ways. Rather than portraying these fans strictly as cultural resistors who strove to challenge what mass media and society was offering them, the texts they created instead reveal that many fan communities hoped to cultivate partnerships with the industry in ways that would benefit both sides.

This study also weaves together conversations in fan studies with dialogues surrounding music criticism and reception. Throughout the history of music criticism, the source material generally published in the public sphere and studied by musicologists tends to be written by males. This of course parallels the history of Western music itself, as well as musical canon formation, and continues to be an increasingly prominent discussion within

---

[7] Henry Jenkins and John Tulloch, *Science Fiction Audiences: Watching "Doctor Who" and "Star Trek"* (London: Routledge, 1995), 23.

[8] Francesca Coppa, "Fuck Yeah, Fandom Is Beautiful," *Journal of Fandom Studies* 2, no. 1 (2014): 78.

[9] Suzanne Scott, *Fake Geek Girls: Fandom, Gender, and the Convergence Culture Industry* (New York: New York University Press, 2019).

the field of musicology. One of the most notable studies of this gendered paradigm is Marcia J. Citron's *Gender and the Musical Canon*, which prompts us to ask questions about music reception that are not typically answered in traditional music criticism. For example, how do less tangible factors such as pleasure affect music reception? What exactly is a music critic and what do they do? How can we further understand the reception of female audiences if, as Citron explains, "Whether it be for teaching or entertainment, or the parlor or the music club, female interpretive communities have typically operated outside the mainstream and beyond the reach of the professional critic"?[10] The answers to these questions lie in looking outside of formal music criticism to those texts and objects created by female audiences themselves, a method we can borrow from the first wave of fan studies.

Sources and Fan Demographics

This book recreates 1940s American teenage cultures primarily through examining texts and objects created by wartime teens from both inside and outside of popular music fan communities. These include fan club journals, which were authored, printed, and distributed entirely by fan club members; fan mail and personal correspondence between fan club members; and reader write-ins to commercially published fan magazines. It is important to note that while these sources reveal unprecedented insight into the teenage communities featured in this study, there are certain limits and challenges that they entail, as is the case with most studies of material culture.

This particular study of teen fan communities in the 1940s and the source material used is limited for the most part to examining those teen girls who were active participants in fan groups. This is due on the one hand to the source material featured, which was created by these active fans, and on the other, because it is important not to overlook specific female fan communities that created their own worlds and cultural practices in favor of larger, more general audiences because these fan communities reveal much about the cultural environments they were surrounded by. Nevertheless, it is worth noting that the primary source material used in this book does not reflect what life was like for every American teenage girl or those who were more

---

[10] Marcia J. Citron, *Gender and the Musical Canon* (Cambridge: Cambridge University Press, 1993), 188.

casual followers of Frank Sinatra and other popular icons. Rather, they create a picture of how popular music and culture affected the cultural experiences of those teenage girls who prioritized their own participation in it.

Similarly, these sources do not always provide specific information about ethnicity, class, or overall socioeconomic backgrounds of the members of these fan communities. While names, ages, interests, and contact information of club members were often included in fan club journals and correspondence, it is difficult to pinpoint more specific demographic information about the "typical" club member. This should be considered alongside an important concern that has been receiving increasing attention in fan studies, that is, an overwhelming tendency to consider fandom and fan studies through a white lens. Mel Stanfill brings this issue to light most clearly, indicating a need for scholars in fan studies to not ignore race in favor of only gender, or only class, or any other singular factor. As Stanfill explains, by not naming a fan community as predominantly white if that is the case, scholars reinforce the implication that racially unidentified fandoms are inherently understood as white, creating intersectional gaps if other factors such as gender, class, and sexuality are considered independently of race and ethnicity.[11]

In terms of the Frank Sinatra fans featured in this book, certain elements of their fan club practices suggest that most club members were probably white, as does popular memory's representations of 1940s bobbysoxers in general. Fan club journals often featured member profiles, which usually listed member names, ages, and interests, but did not mention race or ethnicity. However, indications that many members attended high school and had enough extra time and income to participate in extracurricular activities such as music classes and attending movies and concerts suggest a middle-to-upper-class membership and opportunities most often available to white youth.

As this book will explore, however, it is not as easy to assume that most Sinatra fan club members were white and economically privileged as it may initially appear, although multiple indicators do suggest this. Chapter 3, for example, takes an in-depth look into Sinatra's own identity as an Italian American and the perception he created that he came from working-class roots (which was somewhat true, though his family did not suffer as much as many others did during the Great Depression), and how this identity and

---

[11] Mel Stanfill, "The Unbearable Whiteness of Fandom and Fan Studies," in *A Companion to Media Fandom and Fan Studies*, ed. Paul Booth (Hoboken, NJ: John Wiley and Sons, 2018), 310.

Sinatra's public speaking regarding racial and religious tolerance worked to encourage a more diverse fan base than more conventionally white stars, such as Bing Crosby, may have. This aspect of Sinatra's celebrity identity led to activity within his fans' clubs that worked to similarly promote ideals of tolerance as well as liberal politics. These practices of course do not prove that Sinatra fan clubs had significantly diverse membership. But the specific values these clubs held, combined with the fact that members could participate at any level of anonymity they chose, as will be discussed in Chapter 2, suggest a potentially more inclusive fan community when compared to other celebrity fan groups of the era.

It is also important to note that anonymity within fandom does not automatically create colorblind communities, as Stanfill warns, yet it is equally important to note that Sinatra fan club members were generally not asked to provide any personal information for membership consideration outside of affirmation that they admired Sinatra.[12] Additionally, many Sinatra fan clubs had wide, geographically diverse membership, and many club members never met each other in person at all, instead relying on fan club journals and letters to connect with one another.

Determining fan club member demographics based on class, employment status, and high school enrollment is also more nuanced during World War II than we may assume. It is true that youth of working-class families were required and expected to work more often than youth of middle- and upper-class families out of economic necessity, suggesting that leisure activities such as fan club participation was more accessible to middle- and upper-class youth. As Chapters 1 and 3 will explore, however, factors such as the Fair Labor Standards Act of 1938, recovery from the Great Depression, and the wartime challenges that African Americans (and African American women especially) faced finding employment complicate this assumption. Again, these factors do not immediately point to diverse fan club membership, but the abrupt changes within the World War II working sphere combined with Sinatra's public identity as a celebrity with working-class, Italian American roots creates space to consider potentially wider demographics in Sinatra fan communities when compared to those of other celebrities.

With these limits in mind, the fan-made source materials featured in this study nevertheless work to reconstruct in exciting detail the communities that American teenage girls built around popular culture. Highlighting these

[12] Stanfill, "Unbearable Whiteness," 309.

girls as cultural producers reveals a dynamic World War II social group that proved to value professionalism, productivity, and connection in their lives, even in the midst of international chaos.

Chapter Overview

Chapter 1 prefaces this examination by setting the scene of cultural forces that affected and shaped American girl culture during the 1940s. Just as they are today, both women and girls were pressured to maintain particular beauty and hygiene standards, which were set by an ever-growing cosmetics industry. While advertisements encouraged young females to strive for beauty and allurement, the government and other areas of society complicated expectations by distributing contradictory messages regarding female roles and sexuality. Yes, women were encouraged to take on war work, but the expectation that they would return to domestic lives once the war was over ran alongside these recruitment efforts. Older teens and younger women were expected to maintain conventional beauty standards, even as they took on roles as industrial workers and military personnel, to maintain appropriate levels of femininity and maintain male morale. Sexual promiscuity, however, was discouraged. But on the other hand, American servicemen needed morale boosts whenever possible, and American women were expected to provide these "boosts" as an act of patriotism. As Marilyn E. Hegarty writes, American women and girls were facing "a veritable catch-22" in the realm of sexual expectations.[13] The contradictions go on, and it is not difficult to see why younger teenage girls might have grappled with uncertainty about their roles and futures as American women within this climate.

Chapter 2 shifts focus to the social organizations American teens created around popular music. Already a distinct social and consumer group due to the dramatic increase in high school attendance from the 1930s into the 1940s, teenagers who desired to further their sense of community with peers engaged in Teen Canteens, local spaces where both boys and girls could gather after school to dance, listen to music, socialize, and pursue opportunities to contribute to the war effort. Despite the success of Teen Canteens, efforts within these organizations to diversify membership and

---

[13] Marilyn E. Hegarty, *Victory Girls, Khaki-Wackies, and Patriotutes: The Regulation of Female Sexuality during World War II* (New York: New York University Press, 2008), 85.

model ideals of democracy were met with varying levels of success, and some were forced to shut down due to conflicts surrounding racial intolerance and fears regarding interactions between boys and girls. Chapter 2 then moves into a detailed look into the world of Frank Sinatra fan clubs, the membership of which was primarily teenage girls. This prompts questions regarding why teenage girls sought their own spaces outside of organizations like Teen Canteens, what they got out of them, and what teenage girls were able to do within the relative safety of these communities that they couldn't do in public.

Chapter 3 explores how Sinatra fans used their fan communities to bring their voices into the public sphere on issues such as civil rights and politics. Taking a cue from Sinatra's public work against racial and religious discrimination and his willingness to share the prejudices he faced as an Italian American, his teen fans worked to spread similar messages of tolerance and discussed these ideas within their clubs. While teenage girls were generally low on the proverbial totem pole of American society when it came to having their voices and opinions taken seriously (demonstrated by such portrayals as the hysterical hens in *Swooner Crooner*), media sources suggest that as a group, teen girls in fact held a certain level of perceived power when it came to influencing the future directions America would take in addressing civil rights and politics.

In addition to their public efforts on the home front, teenage Sinatra fans cultivated international relationships with foreign Sinatra fans. These fan relationships were encouraged by Sinatra's fan club coordinator and liaison, Marjorie Diven, who founded an organization called the Adopt a Foreign Fan Association (AAFFA). Clubs that were members of the AAFFA were given names and addresses of foreign fans that could be distributed among club members who wanted to begin international pen-pal relationships. Operating in the middle of international conflict and nationalist mindsets, the attitudes Sinatra's teenage fans displayed toward embracing internationalism reached far beyond the stereotypes society placed on them.

Chapter 4 moves the discussion inward to explore how teenage girls interacted with popular music within their fan club communities. Looking back to the questions Marcia J. Citron prompts regarding the history of music criticism, this chapter considers the female fans of Frank Sinatra as music critics. Both in commercial fan magazines such as *Modern Screen* and in Frank Sinatra fan club journals, teenage girls recorded their opinions on cultural topics using many different formats, including what we might consider traditional, review-based music criticism, but also original poetry, reenactments, essays, and artwork. In Frank Sinatra fan clubs, fans even developed their own unique ways of recording elements of Sinatra's musical style in prose.

Chapter 5 examines the cultural shifts that took place both in America at large and within Sinatra's fan communities after World War II ended. Teenage girls, who were either nearing or had already entered adulthood, were now facing the same questions many young women across the country were. Namely, if women had taken on roles in the workforce during the war, would they be able to continue in those roles? Should they give them up to men returning from overseas? Would teenage girls who did not hold jobs during the war be able to start one, or had expectations shifted back to prewar life, when the main priority of young white women leaving school was to pursue marriage and family life? Would the ideals of democracy that the United States preached in contrast to the fascism of the Axis powers really prevail, and would girls from working-class and non-white backgrounds truly be able to experience the sense of hope and opportunity many white women were experiencing, or even be able to live the suburban lifestyle many white Americans would strive for? The postwar years both answered and complicated these questions.

Frank Sinatra also experienced extreme personal changes after the war's end. While his vulnerable performance persona continued to show up in some of his postwar work, particularly in films such as *On the Town* (MGM 1949), Sinatra's personal life was leading to the dramatic shift in persona he would adopt in the late 1940s and early 1950s – —that of the womanizing, Jack Daniels–drinking saloon singer—that he was known as for decades to follow.

The book concludes by once again considering historical remembrance. The past decade has seen large-scale cultural responses to what would have been Frank Sinatra's one hundredth birthday in 2015 and the seventy-fifth anniversary of the end of World War II in 2020. In Sinatra's case, these celebrations represented Sinatra largely as the masculine idol he transformed into starting in the 1950s, with tributes to his days in the Rat Pack and his later hit songs, such as "My Way." This image was influenced in part by shifting perceptions of Sinatra's Italian American identity, which during World War II marked him as potentially dangerous for teenage girls, but in the 1950s contributed to a new image of masculinity, albeit one that was often associated with crime. Recent memorials of World War II have included tributes and images dedicated to Americans who fought overseas and the many women who took on roles in the workforce in their absence, with "Rosie the Riveter" persisting as the ultimate icon of the war-era American women.

Sinatra's early career in the 1940s as well as images of American youth during World War II have been largely absent from these historical remembrances. Frank Sinatra's early influence on American society, however, and the material culture produced by American teenage girls in response provide a new narrative in the history of American youth culture, World War II, and popular music. By highlighting unacknowledged voices of female youth, we discover new challenges and uncertainty teenage girls faced during the war, and even more significantly, the creative and passionate contributions they made to the development of American popular culture.

1
Teenage Girls in Wartime American Culture

The United States cannot hold itself aloof from the present war, and must devote its full powers, moral, military and economic to the defeat of the Axis powers.... We must take our part in devising and establishing a new world order in which lawless aggression will be impossible and in which the countries that strive for a free and democratic way of life may be at peace.[1]

Such was the tone of hundreds of newspaper articles in the days following December 7, 1941, after Pearl Harbor was bombed by the Imperial Japanese Navy and Franklin D. Roosevelt declared the United States to be in a state of war. Overnight, American life shifted from relative normalcy and distance from the war in Europe to an unprecedented united feeling of anger. Americans wanted to take action in a way they never did during World War I and the early years of World War II, and they seemed to readily agree with their president when he spoke on behalf of them, saying, "I believe that I interpret the will of the Congress and of the people when I assert that we will not only defend ourselves to the uttermost, but will make it very certain that this form of treachery shall never again endanger us."[2]

History remembers World War II as a major turning point in almost all facets of American culture, but especially in how citizens who were previously excluded from the mainstream public sphere—namely, women and minority groups—suddenly found themselves in both civilian and military working roles that had been closed to them. Almost overnight, the US government had to try to convince a nation of segregation, strict gender roles, and immigrants that everyone was an American and had a duty to work together to fight fascism. Not an easy or always genuine task, as we will see, but one that impacted American society for decades to follow and was ultimately

---

[1] Payson S. Wild, "This Is a Global War," *Daily Boston Globe*, December 9, 1941, 18.
[2] Franklin D. Roosevelt, "December 7, 1941: A Date Which Will Live in Infamy" (Address to Congress, December 8, 1941).

supported by a colossal partnership system between the US government, corporations, entertainment industry, and advertising industry.[3]

In the narratives of American women's history, it is easy to find a wealth of scholarship, fiction, films, television shows, and music about the incredible ways women adapted to and succeeded in the new roles they took on during World War II, including industrial work and joining the armed forces.[4] And although this representation performs the important role of highlighting a hugely significant time for American women, there remains a lack in historical representation of what life was like for those women who were too young to participate full-time in the workforce, yet old enough to feel a desire to contribute to the war effort. For American teenage girls, World War II was not necessarily the liberating experience it was for those women who were willing and able to join the public work sphere. Instead, the war brought uncertainties to teenage girls who were trying to define a sense of purpose and expectations for themselves and their futures. This chapter examines the challenges teenage girls faced as wartime Americans and the contradictory messaging regarding female roles and sexuality they received from advertisements, the US government, and society in general. In addition, highlighting the female fans and celebrity persona of Frank Sinatra demonstrates how the interconnectedness of the entertainment industry and propaganda during World War II simultaneously fueled feelings of freedom and restriction in the lives of teenage girls.

Women and War

World War II marked one of the most significant eras in the history of American women's transition from being expected to hold primarily domestic homemaking roles to becoming active members of the public sphere. Following important moments such as the women's suffrage movement and earned right to vote in 1920, World War II was a crucial moment that revealed American women to be not only perfectly capable of fulfilling public roles usually reserved for men, but absolutely necessary to the success of the

---

[3] For more on the shifts in American culture during World War II, see Lewis A. Erenberg and Susan E. Hirsch, eds., *The War in American Culture: Society and Consciousness During World War II* (Chicago: University of Chicago Press, 1996).

[4] Female branches of the US military during World War II included the Nurse Corps, Women's Army Corps, Marine Corps Women's Reserves, and others.

war as members of the public workforce. While American women took on a variety of new roles during the war, three primary areas proved particularly significant in the advancement of women's opportunities. These were nursing, military roles, and industry roles.

World War II scholar Doris Weatherford notes that in 1940, before America's official entry into World War II, the Army Nurse Corps included about 700 female nurses. As it became clear that America would need to start planning for potential involvement in the war, that number skyrocketed to about 700 new nurses every month by April 1941.[5] Nursing proved to be one of the most necessary and heavily recruited for roles for American women throughout the war, with new recruits constantly sought after as the need for nurses continued to increase.

As part of these recruiting efforts, the US and state governments enacted certain incentives to try to convince young women to train as nurses. The Bolton Bill, for example, passed in May 1943, worked to provide financial support for women in nursing school and created the Student Nurse Corps. The bill and its incentives were intended to be advertised both to older nurses who needed refresher courses or were interested in further nursing education and young women just entering the field. High school counselors in many states were encouraged to discuss the bill and other similar programs with high school girls in an effort to move more female high school graduates into nursing programs.[6] These kinds of programs and recruiting efforts proved to open a significant number of new educational opportunities for women and high school–aged girls who may not have been able to pursue higher education before the war.

In addition to an increasing need for trained nurses, all branches of the US military similarly recognized a need for more manpower, or in this case womanpower, as the war progressed. While women did participate as members of the armed forces during America's involvement in World War I—though not all military branches included women—this involvement ended shortly after the armistice.[7] Permanent opportunities for women in the military were not established until World War II.

By the beginning of 1943, all branches of the US military had established women's divisions. Bearing memorable acronyms such as WAACs

---

[5] Doris Weatherford, *American Women and World War II* (Edison, NJ: Castle Books, 2008), 16.
[6] Weatherford, *American Women and World War II*, 17.
[7] For more information on American women's involvement in World War I, see Lettie Gavin, *American Women in World War I: They Also Served* (Niwot: University Press of Colorado, 1997).

(Women's Army Auxiliary Corps, later WACs), WAVES (Women Accepted for Volunteer Emergency Service), and SPARs (Semper Paratus—Always Ready), these women's divisions created thousands of opportunities for women to aid in the war effort, and they were eager to join. All branches were overrun with applications to join as the war ramped up. For example, at one point the army received 13,000 applications in a single day from American women for just 450 available officer candidate positions. Enlistment goals for women were hit in all branches, despite rather strict enlistment requirements when compared to American men. In almost all women's branches of the armed forces, candidates were required to have at least completed their high school education, with some branches such as the WAVES requiring women to have a college degree or "over two years of college work plus at least two years' professional or business experience applicable to naval jobs," and preferred women who "majored in engineering, astronomy, meteorology, electronics, physics, mathematics, metallurgy, business statistics and modern foreign languages."[8] While other women's branches did not require as much education as the navy, most still required that women enlistees be over twenty or twenty-one years of age (depending on the branch), while American men were required to be eighteen to enlist.

It is important to acknowledge here that while the war opened so many new roles for women, not all women experienced these shifts in the same, positive way. Women from working-class backgrounds and African American women especially—many of whom were already working out of necessity before World War II in often low-level jobs—had to simultaneously confront new opportunities and restrictions in the working sphere. Sherrie Tucker makes this important point, noting that while "over 400,000 black women were able to leave domestic work for higher paying factory jobs," popular images of what the new American working woman supposedly looked like were not representative of their experiences. Rather, these images emphasized a kind of housewife-to-factory narrative and the contributions of white women who were entering the workforce for the first time.[9]

One of the most recognizable images of American women's involvement in World War II is that of "Rosie the Riveter," a strong yet conventionally attractive, white woman with her boiler suit sleeve rolled up indicating her role as a wartime factory worker. While the most famous image of Rosie,

---

[8] Weatherford, *American Women and World War II*, 31–32.
[9] Sherrie Tucker, *Swing Shift: "All-Girl" Bands of the 1940s* (Durham, NC: Duke University Press, 2001), 19.

Figure 1.1 "We Can Do It!" J. Howard Miller. 1942. National Museum of American History.

painted by J. Howard Miller in 1942 as a recruiting tool for Westinghouse (Figure 1.1), was not actually distributed all that widely during the actual war years,[10] this image proved in the following decades to influence collective memory into remembering American women's entry into industry as one of the primary ways they contributed to the war effort and altered the trajectory of women's roles in the public sphere after the war's end.[11] Yet as authors such as Maureen Honey have highlighted, this image and others worked to erase the contributions of wartime working-class and African American women in popular memory, reinforcing practices of segregation and discrimination in the workforce even as the United States touted

---

[10] Michelle Smith, "In Rosie's Shadow: World War II Recruitment Rhetoric and Women's Work in Public Memory," in *Women at Work: Rhetorics of Gender and Labor*, ed. David Gold and Jessica Enoch (Pittsburgh: University of Pittsburgh Press, 2019), 186.

[11] Doris Weatherford, *American Women during World War II: An Encyclopedia* (New York: Routledge, 2010), 399–400.

messages of the necessity for all women to join the war effort.[12] Despite the desperate need for workers, employment patterns in World War II America were still segregated, and employers often required that black workers use separate facilities, or just did not hire them at all.[13] And even when black women were hired, their contributions to the war effort were generally not acknowledged.

Considering the contributions of all American women during the war—not just those whom print media portrayed as the ideal white, middle-class female worker—makes clear the fact that America would not have achieved the success it did in World War II had it not been for the tireless efforts of women who worked to build the supplies necessary for victory and supported the war in a variety of other ways. As Weatherford writes, "When President Roosevelt asked in 1940 for 50,000 planes a year, his political opponents saw this impossible goal as clear evidence that he had gone mad, but by 1944 the United States was producing 120,000 planes annually. Many of these aircraft were built in plants where more than half of the employees were female."[14] Similar to the increasing roles created for women as nurses and members of the armed forces, industry work not only provided American women with opportunities to earn money independently, but also provided new educational opportunities in which they could learn and develop skill sets they could apply to potential work after the war's end, although conflicting messages regarding the expectations of American women upon the return of servicemen persisted.

While nursing, military roles, and industry work were not the only ways American women could contribute to the war effort, these three areas represented the most drastic shifts in opportunities for women, both as wage earners and students. And while the contributions of these women have been rightfully acknowledged and emphasized in American women's history, this leads to questions about how America's younger women—specifically, teenage girls—who were not quite old enough to pursue such opportunities navigated the war and their place within it.

---

[12] Maureen Honey, *Bitter Fruit: African American Women in World War II* (Columbia: University of Missouri Press, 1999), 2.
[13] Honey, *Bitter Fruit*, 8.
[14] Weatherford, *American Women and World War II*, 116.

Contradictions and Cosmetics: The Challenge of Conflicting Expectations in Teen Girl Culture

In his study of early twentieth-century youth culture, Jon Savage summarizes the predicament many American teenage girls found themselves in during World War II, writing, "Life was hard for females under the conscription age of twenty: as one complained, 'Being sixteen or seventeen, we're considered too young for the armed forces and too young for work in war factories.' With no immediate part to play, and with the disappearance of many male contemporaries, the result was 'a continual sense of frustration.'"[15] To further examine the frustration many American teenagers, and especially teenage girls, were facing during World War II, it is helpful to briefly step back and understand how American teenage culture developed into what it became during the 1940s. The term "teenager" was still relatively new at the beginning of the war years, developing primarily from an increase in commercial marketing tactics directed toward youth as a distinct consumer group. Before the Great Depression, American youth were not seen as an autonomous cultural group as they were from around the mid-twentieth century on. With fewer adolescents completing high school and more entering the workforce at earlier ages in the early twentieth century, American teens were viewed more as young members of adult society rather than a unique consumer and cultural group.

As America entered the Great Depression, however, more American youth were encouraged to remain in school longer to free up as many jobs as possible for adults, increasing high school attendance significantly. Many youth continued to hold part-time employment, especially those from working-class backgrounds who needed to work out of necessity for their families. However, measures such as the Fair Labor Standards Act of 1938, which mandated that children under the age of fourteen could only work at family-owned businesses or farms and children under sixteen could not work during school hours, contributed to a dramatic increase in high school attendance throughout the country. In addition, all children under eighteen were not allowed to work jobs that were deemed hazardous by the secretary of labor.[16]

---

[15] Jon Savage, *Teenage: The Prehistory of Youth Culture, 1875–1945* (London: Penguin, 2007), 404.
[16] Fair Labor Standards Act of 1938.

These combined factors led to an increase in American high school enrollment from 10.6 percent in 1900 to 71.3 percent by 1940.[17] As the economy began to recover after the Depression, this new and much larger demographic of high school–aged Americans began to spend money and demonstrate consumer preferences specific to their ages and cultural practices, something American companies were quick to recognize. Advertisers began marketing products targeted directly to this group, addressing them as "teeners," "teensters," and by around 1941, "teenagers."[18]

Because of factors including the Fair Labor Standards Act of 1938 and higher age minimums for women to enter the military, American teenage girls were left in the background of wartime society when women began entering public work in large numbers at the war's start. Teenage girls were encouraged to contribute to the war effort as best they could, for example by helping with wartime rationing, tending to victory gardens, volunteering for local aid organizations, and taking on some part-time work. But while many girls dutifully worked at these important tasks, the concrete feeling of accomplishment and community that came with working full-time in a war factory or enlisting was notably absent for some, as Savage notes. In addition, teenage girls felt uncertain as to what their postwar lives might look like. On the one hand, the female work revolution of the war years brought excitement for younger girls who hoped to pursue a career in their adult life, suggesting there was a possible alternative to staying at home. On the other hand, while propaganda encouraged women's work using images such as the "Rosie the Riveter" figure, society simultaneously reiterated to women that this work was temporary, fueling the expectation that women would return to the domestic sphere when the war was over. As a result, teenage girls were encouraged to set their sights on future war work yet maintain a domestic education to prepare for a return to postwar "normalcy."

Further complicating the lives of American teenage girls was the steady stream of contradictory messaging coming from families, mass media, and the US government regarding female sexuality. Apparent especially in fan magazines such as *Modern Screen* (1930–1985), *Screenland* (1920–1971), *Photoplay* (1911–1980), and *Radio Mirror* (1933–1977), girls were subjected

---

[17] Kelly Schrum, *Some Wore Bobby Sox: The Emergence of Teenage Girls' Culture, 1920–1945* (New York: Palgrave Macmillan, 2004), 12.
[18] Kathryn H. Fuller, *At the Picture Show: Small-Town Audiences and the Creation of Movie Fan Culture* (Washington, DC: Smithsonian Institution Press, 1996), 145–148.

to dizzying amounts of advertising, just as they are today, that encouraged seemingly ideal standards of sexuality, beauty, and patriotism. These ideals, however, were not consistent. Fan magazines, which catered primarily to teenage girls and young women, contained overwhelming amounts of advertisements that largely promoted two kinds of general lifestyles: (1) conservative lifestyles that emphasized futures as domestic and patriotic homemakers, and (2) lifestyles that emphasized feminine beauty, dating, and fun.

An example of a common wartime ad campaign that promoted a domestic and patriotic lifestyle was for Camay soap. Camay ads could be found in almost every issue of major fan magazines like *Modern Screen* and *Photoplay*. Most Camay ads featured an illustration of a young woman wearing a wedding dress and veil with a (likely fabricated) product review from the bride. The August 1943 issue of *Modern Screen* includes a Camay ad featuring "Mrs. Thomas Allen Smith, of Larchmont, N.Y.," who allegedly claims, "I made my own test of the Camay Mild-Soap Diet. And my!—how much clearer and more velvety my skin seems" (Figure 1.2). The obvious suggestion in Camay ads that use of their soap would lead to the ultimate goal of marriage for young women was also accompanied by suggestions that proper use of their soap could aid the war effort. The same ad that features Mrs. Thomas Allen Smith includes advice on how to make a bar of soap last as long as possible in order to "Save for War!" Ads like these that promoted standardized beauty, marriage, and domestic patriotism were common during the war and supported an ideal image of mainstream American life that citizens were encouraged to defend and emulate.

In contrast, some ads in these same magazines seemed to support fun and romance with multiple partners, a kind of lifestyle that American traditions and much of adult society condemned, especially while the country was at war. Ads for Ipana toothpaste, which appeared just as frequently as Camay ads, tended to promote this lifestyle. One Ipana ad in the July 1944 issue of *Photoplay*, which is notably located directly across from a typical Camay ad, demonstrates this by featuring a modern, young, working woman who enjoys an exciting nightlife (Figure 1.3). The ad, of which the headline provocatively states that "After Hours—hearts are drawn to a bright, sparkling smile!," claims that healthy teeth are key to being "popular" with romantic partners. Rather than depicting an image of a bride, the ad shows an independent woman against a backdrop of the various working roles she is capable of, such as factory work, nursing, and farming. Rather than promoting

Figure 1.2 Ad for Camay soap in *Modern Screen*. August 1943. Media History Digital Library.

patriotism through domestic rationing as in Camay ads, this Ipana ad encourages women to take on work in the public sphere, saying,

> You'll celebrate Victory with a clear conscience. Because you're working hard toward it now. Good girl. After hours, you rate the best in fun and romance!
>
> So powder your nose—and smile. Go out and have FUN! That smile, now—how'd it look in the mirror? Did it sparkle? Was it bright and captivating?
>
> *That's* the kind of smile that turns heads and hearts! If you'll notice, most popular girls aren't beautiful at all. But they all have a beautiful smile!

While these two contrasting advertisement practices may initially appear to be providing teenage girls with options for how they may choose to pursue their lives, the reality was one of uncertainty for many girls who were further influenced by families and society outside the entertainment industry. As Kathy

Figure 1.3 Ad for Ipana toothpaste in *Photoplay*. July 1944. Media History Digital Library.

Peiss writes in her study of American beauty culture, "Where to draw the line—between proper grooming and unseemly glamorizing, between children's make-believe and adult makeup—vexed parents, schools, and manufacturers. Girls were taught the lesson of better appearance through cosmetics, yet cautioned against looking too sexual and mature."[19] For every Ipana ad that encouraged fun and independence (alongside body self-consciousness), there

---

[19] Kathy Peiss, *Hope in a Jar: The Making of America's Beauty Culture* (Philadelphia: University of Pennsylvania Press, 2011), 252.

was a voice elsewhere that reminded women and girls that a return to prewar domesticity was expected once the war ended. Even within many magazines, articles and features that were published alongside these ads offered unending advice to teenage girls that demonstrated highly contradictory expectations, sometimes within the very same regular feature.

One recurring feature that claimed to offer relatable advice to teenage girls was found in *Ladies' Home Journal*. Although the magazine's primary readership was adult women, a column entitled "the Sub-Deb" was introduced in 1928. Kelly Schrum notes that this column was originally intended for upper-middle-class girls, "girls with plans for college, debutante balls, or marriage."[20] The column shifted direction in 1931 with the onset of a new editor, Elizabeth Woodward, offering more casual advice to a wider demographic of teenage girls on topics such as dating, school, and home life. While the column initially appears to try to relate to teenage girls by discussing these everyday topics and using slang, reading through multiple issues of the column reveals that double standards and contradictory expectations for American girls and boys were strongly reinforced.

Two representative examples can be found in the April and December 1944 issues of *Ladies' Home Journal*. The April 1944 column, simply titled, "No!," is meant to provide teenage girls with ways they can stop advancing men who "want more" than girls should give them. While the advice delivers a bad taste for modern readers, placing most of the responsibility of sexual restraint in a relationship on women and equating premarital sex with shame, it at least offers girls an alternative to the societal narrative of "helping" servicemen in any way possible (Figure 1.4). Just eight months later in December 1944, however, the column provides very different advice, this time directed at boys. This column is subtly titled "How to be Devastating to Women" and provides such advice tidbits as, "For your first date, pick a girl who's had her first date.... You don't want a strange dead weight to drag while you're trying something new," and "women are your object. You're not at all interested in getting stuck with one. Not until you've had a chance to look them all over. It's the field for you. Playing the game with all women" (Figure 1.5). The double standards highlighted in these two columns are not hard to see and were present throughout "the Sub-Deb" in the 1940s. Schrum summarizes the contradictory nature of columns like these during the war, which advised girls to "focus on attracting and pleasing boys but to avoid

---

[20] Schrum, *Some Wore Bobby Sox*, 15.

Figure 1.4 "The Sub-Deb" column in *Ladies' Home Journal*. April 1944. ProQuest Women's Magazine Archive.

becoming 'boy crazy' or too serious about one boyfriend," and to "Learn to be sexually appealing to boys ... but not too sexy or too sexually active; flirt, but do not flirt too much; be coy, but be yourself.[21]

---

[21] Schrum, *Some Wore Bobby Sox*, 17.

Figure 1.5 "The Sub-Deb" column in *Ladies' Home Journal*. December 1944. ProQuest Women's Magazine Archive.

Conflicting guidelines regarding female sexuality were notably not restricted to entertainment and commercial media like fan and women's magazines. The US government was concerned enough with female sexuality during the war to devise federal guidelines on how women should manage their sexuality in a way that was intended to aid the war effort and both serve and protect male military personnel.

Marilyn E. Hegarty's study of World War II regulations of female sexuality provides a revealing look into the complex web of myths, expectations, and contradictions surrounding America's perspective of sex during the war. American women faced expectations to remain faithful to their men serving overseas alongside a rampant national belief that women were the primary spreaders of venereal diseases. At the same time, there was an underlying belief in American society that servicemen needed sex to maintain morale, and American women should be willing to provide it. In Hegarty's words, "Prostitution was illegal, promiscuity was immoral, female sexuality was dangerous, but sexual labor was essential to the war effort—a veritable catch-22."[22]

While it was expected that American women provide such moral support if requested by an American serviceman, the United States simultaneously implemented government mandates in an attempt to control the spread of venereal diseases, which proved crippling for the military. The May Act, for example, was passed in 1941 and criminalized prostitution that occurred within a certain distance of military establishments. Government decrees regarding venereal disease in the military overwhelmingly pinpointed female prostitutes as the primary spreaders and greatest risk to servicemen's health. The health of prostitutes themselves, or the question of how they contracted these diseases in the first place, was conveniently overlooked.[23]

The accusation that females were primarily at fault for the serious venereal disease problem facing the US military was not limited to adult women. Teenage girls were also subjected to this message. An example appears in a 1945 academic study titled "The Venereal Disease Problem in the United States in World War II," in which author William L. Fleming lists certain challenges still facing the fight against venereal disease:

> The Army has discovered that the lowering of its venereal disease rate by the campaign against prostitution has been partly offset by an increase in

---

[22] Marilyn E. Hegarty, *Victory Girls, Khaki-Wackies, and Patriotutes: The Regulation of Female Sexuality during World War II* (New York: New York University Press, 2008), 85.
[23] For an overview of government attitudes and actions towards war-era prostitution and venereal disease, see Eliot Ness's article, "Federal Government's Program in Attacking the Problem of Prostitution," *Federal Probation* (April–June 1943).

infections due to pick-ups, waitresses, tavern and dance hall girls, and the life, who at most are only part-time prostitutes and many of whom are teenage girls.[24]

The implied equating of unmarried sex with prostitution coupled with media advice on both attracting and avoiding men left American teenage girls in a moral conundrum that was further fueled by expectations that they maintain conventional standards of beauty. Among this push-and-pull, it is notable that there were instances when female youth defended themselves and the rampant generalizations regarding the dangers of female sexuality. In one 1944 *New York Times Article*, "As the Youngsters See Juvenile Delinquency," the author quotes a seventeen-year-old girl who supposedly summed up the opinion of "thousands of young people" when she said:

> The rise in juvenile delinquency among girls has been particularly emphasized, referring especially to promiscuous sex relations, venereal disease, and pregnancy. That's not delinquency; that's really serious. But adults should stop and think before they call the majority of girls immoral. For instance, you read and hear much about young girls walking arm in arm with sailors and soldiers. I do that every time my brother comes home on furlough. I have seen adults look at me as if I were a juvenile delinquent. Several times I have wanted to call out "It may interest you to know that I am walking with my brother and that after the show we are going home where we shall be with our family."[25]

Despite these instances of self-defense, it is not difficult to imagine the kinds of questions these girls were grappling with. If premarital sex was immoral, how should teenage girls respond to advances by soldiers, whom girls were generally told they should support unconditionally? Why should teenage girls work to make themselves physically attractive if premarital sex was to be avoided? And perhaps most significant, how should teenage girls deal with their own sexual feelings if there was a taboo on female sexual expression outside of marriage and the private domestic sphere? For many

---

[24] William L. Fleming, "The Venereal Disease Problem in the United States in World War II," *Journal of the Elisha Mitchell Scientific Society* 61, no. 1/2 (August 1945): 199.

[25] Dorothy Gordon, "As the Youngsters See Juvenile Delinquency: They Think Grown-ups Misjudge the Causes and Propose Some Measures of Their Own," *New York Times*, August 6, 1944, 16.

girls, and to the chagrin of many adults, the answer to this last question appeared in part through adoration of the decade's newest, and in some ways least popular pop idol, Frank Sinatra.

"Then All Semblance of Order Vanished": Media Representations of American Masculinity, Frank Sinatra, and His Young Female Fans

The response of the entertainment industry to America's entrance into World War II was one of swift transition to war-focused and patriotic content. Many entertainment writers, producers, and stars felt their jobs were as essential to the war effort as those of the government and military. Just two weeks after America declared war on Japan, *Billboard* magazine published a feature illustrating the role they envisioned entertainment would play in the war:

> We in the show business have a double duty. Wars are won not only by armies and navies, by tanks and planes and anti-aircraft guns, but, above all, by morale. And the show business is the greatest single force in national life capable of maintaining the morale of the entire nation.... We must bring to the people those brief interludes of escape and momentary happiness without which no people can go on; we must provide those strength-giving moments under no matter what conditions may develop. The morale of the nation is, in a large measure, our direct charge. It is a grave, terrible and sacred trust. We have a tremendous job to do, thru what may be long and harrowing years. We can and will do it![26]

While it is challenging to measure if the entertainment industry really was the "greatest single force" available to boost American morale, it is clear the industry was serious in creating a system of stars, narratives, and cultural objects that worked to present seemingly ideal representations of American identity and capabilities.

American celebrity personas of the war era were products of the integration between the entertainment industry, advertising industry, and the US government. The government offered guidelines and perks (most notably tax breaks) to the entertainment industry to promote propaganda through

---

[26] "A Job to Do," *Billboard*, December 20, 1941, 3.

celebrities and advertisements. In return, the hope was that American citizens would emulate the characteristics and narratives of those celebrities deemed ideal Americans by these propagandistic standards.[27] These characteristics included unyielding patriotism, a desire to aid the war effort in any way possible, mainstream values of heterosexual romance and family life, both physical and emotional strength, and whiteness. In the realm of American popular music, it is arguable that no two celebrities publicly embodied these characteristics on the home front more so than Glenn Miller and Bing Crosby.

Miller's active service as a military bandleader and dedication to entertaining troops marked him as one of the most beloved stars of the war. In addition, Miller's image and that of his band aligned with those characteristics listed above that the US government prioritized in media and propaganda. Lewis A. Erenberg writes of Miller's wartime image, "[Miller's] preference for a clean-cut version of American jive and a sanitized conception of American culture worked with the government's policy of military segregation and its decision not to disturb deeply held racial values in a time of war. As a result, Miller's AAF Orchestra was all-white rather than all-American."[28] Similarly, while Bing Crosby did not serve in the military (his age and family status prevented him from being called into service), he devoted his professional work to encouraging the American public to support the military, work hard to keep things running at home, and above all, to buy war bonds. And like Miller, Crosby maintained an image of a clean-cut, family-oriented white male devoted to protecting the mainstream American way of life.

One revealing artifact of World War II American entertainment propaganda is the 1945 short film the *All Star Bond Rally*. Produced by Twentieth Century–Fox as a contribution to the seventh drive for war loans, this film serves as a clear example of how American entertainment and the government often merged into one unit. In fact, the film's director, Max Youngstein, worked as both the coordinator of advertising and publicity for Twentieth Century–Fox and the head of the publicity department for the War Finance Division.

---

[27] For more on the interconnectivity of the US government and entertainment advertising, see Michael S. Sweeney, *Secrets of Victory: The Office of Censorship and the American Press and Radio in World War II* (Chapel Hill: University of North Carolina Press, 2001); and Gerd Horten, *Radio Goes to War: The Cultural Politics of Propaganda during World War II* (Berkeley: University of California Press, 2002).

[28] Lewis A. Erenberg, *Swingin' the Dream: Big Band Jazz and the Rebirth of American Culture* (Chicago: University of Chicago Press, 1998), 202.

A conglomeration of some of the biggest stars of the day, including Bing Crosby, Bob Hope, and Betty Grable, the *All Star Bond Rally* moves through a series of acts vaudeville-style. Advertising and entertainment media were also involved in the film's promotion and published reviews of the film that encouraged readers to not only see it, but to buy war bonds in support. One such review appears in the July 1945 issue of *Modern Screen* magazine, the primary readership of which was teenage girls and young women:

> Naturally, it takes something pretty special to rate such an assemblage of talent. It *is* something pretty special—the Seventh War Bond Drive. And look, kids, there just couldn't be anything more important than War Bonds! Not that white "formal" you saw in the window, or the cute suit with the flirt skirt—or *anything*. Because the war isn't over by a long way. There are still the Japs, and the Japs, remember, are the ones responsible for Bataan and Corregidor and the loss of more American boys than we can bear to think about. So buy all the bonds you possibly can—*please?* ... Those stars give their services, so it looks as if we'd better repay them by buying more bonds than we ever have before. Okay?[29]

The film culminates in an act by Bing Crosby who performs the show's theme song, which not-so-subtly encourages viewers to buy war bonds. The song, written by Jimmy McHugh and Harold Adamson, is credited as the "Bond Rally Song" and uses a repetitive melody, textual alliteration, and driving tempo to enforce the song's primary lyrics, "buy, buy, buy, buy a bond." Crosby's performance style is reflective of his overall war-era celebrity persona. He stands tall as if at attention, looks directly into the camera, moves his body very little, and sings with a strong and clear baritone voice. Simply put, he exhibits strength in his performance, which he did throughout his wartime career. Personas of strength, both physical and emotional, were highly valued in America's wartime male stars. Bing Crosby, along with others such as Bob Hope, Humphrey Bogart, Glenn Miller, and Clark Gable, exhibited these characteristics in their celebrity work and came to be seen as seemingly ideal representations of white American masculinity. This leads to questions surrounding one male star who found enormous success during World War II displaying a much different kind of celebrity persona that was characterized not by strength, but vulnerability.

---

[29] Virginia Wilson, "Movie Reviews: Bond Rally," *Modern Screen*, July 1945, 12.

In the same *All Star Bond Rally* that we see a strong and grounded Bing Crosby, we also see a very different performance by Frank Sinatra. While Crosby sings a no-frills rendition of the "Bond Rally Song," Sinatra exhibits a more theatrical performance of "Saturday Night (Is the Loneliest Night of the Week)" by Jule Styne and Sammy Cahn. Whereas Crosby gives a direct performance straight into the camera without any other distractions on stage, Sinatra emerges onto a backlit stage that is framed on either side by Harry James's orchestra. We hear Sinatra before we see him. His voice lacks a body, the very opposite of physical strength. Instead of entering the stage quickly, he slowly meanders, arms swinging, until the camera finally zooms in enough for viewers to see his face. Throughout the performance Sinatra opens his arms, drops them lazily, and sways as he sings a song not of patriotism, but of heartache. This demonstration of vulnerability and a seeming physical lack defined Sinatra's celebrity persona during the years of World War II, which resulted in a duality of inviting scorn from much of adult society and adoration from teenage girls. As Roger Gilbert notes in comparing Crosby and Sinatra, "The fact that two male singers specializing in the same body of material could embody such different modes of cultural value points to a fundamental split in the American character itself." For example, one 1943 article in the *Washington Post* reads:

> The boney pin-up boy of millions of moonstruck girls flunked his Army physical examination today at a Newark induction center. He has a perforated eardrum—self-inflicted by too many renditions of "As Time Goes By," his enemies on Broadway say.... Instead of going on the Army payroll at $50 a month, and eating and equipping himself at the expense of the taxpayers, Sinatra will go back to his swooning audiences and net a million dollars during the next year.[30]

This rather harsh coverage of Sinatra, whom the author describes as the "emaciated Romeo of the Nation's juke box addicts," was relatively typical of press coverage surrounding the star during the war. Sinatra rubbed much of American society the wrong way, primarily because of his appearance, vulnerable performance style, and the fact that he was not called into active duty. At a time when the national imagination envisioned and expected all

---

[30] Bob Considine, "Treasury Gets $880,000 Break, Crooner Sinatra Flunks Draft," *Washington Post*, December 10, 1943, 1.

American men to demonstrate strength and service, many believed Sinatra instead demonstrated weakness and a cushy lifestyle amid national stress. In addition, Sinatra was an Italian American, marking him as less white, and therefore more dangerous, than Crosby.[31] The role of Sinatra's ethnicity in his celebrity identity will be discussed further in Chapter 3, but it is worth noting here that the scrutiny Sinatra faced from certain wartime media sources directed toward his lack of military service, physicality, and above all, his effect on teenage girls, was only aggravated by his Italian American background.

The importance American culture placed on physical male fitness stemmed largely from a desire to reinforce mainstream white masculinity and create an image of American strength for both Allied and Axis countries to see. Christina S. Jarvis's study of American masculinity during World War II explains how although American media and propaganda portrayed the typical white American man as muscular and physically active, the reality of most men was a different story. Jarvis notes that during the Great Depression, "While relatively few Americans actually starved to death, sickness and malnutrition increased dramatically, especially among the unemployed."[32]

It was not easy for many Americans to recover their full health and increase physical fitness after the Great Depression into the 1940s. Toward the beginning of World War II, in fact, the Selective Service reported in July 1941 that of the first one million men examined, 40 percent were deemed unfit for military service and assigned 4-F status. This number climbed to 50 percent by October of the same year.[33] These reports shocked America and led to a variety of large-scale responses, from popular songs like Ted Courtney's "Four-F Charlie," which worked to shame and emasculate those who were deemed physically unfit for service, to advertisement campaigns from food companies claiming their products would improve the diets and physical health of American men.[34] These figures also suggest that while Sinatra was scrutinized for his scrawny appearance, he was in reality much more representative of a typical American man than the more macho

---

[31] For more on the history of American associations of race with danger, especially danger towards women, see Ruth Frankenberg, *White Women, Race Matters: The Social Construction of Whiteness* (Minneapolis: University of Minnesota Press, 1993).

[32] Christina S. Jarvis, *The Male Body at War: American Masculinity during World War II* (DeKalb: Northern Illinois University Press, 2010), 19.

[33] Jarvis, *The Male Body at War*, 60.

[34] Jarvis, *The Male Body at War*, 60–62.

celebrities of the era. The US government did not want to publicize this fact, however, and encouraged the entertainment industry to instead promote male celebrities who exhibited immense physical strength in order to put forward a powerful post-Depression image of the American people to the rest of the world.

Although Sinatra may have been more representative of American physical masculinity than most would have liked to admit, the fact that he was assigned 4-F status for a punctured eardrum (a result of his difficult birth) and was not called into the military—where some men were able to achieve physical transformation—prevented many Americans from feeling sympathetic toward him, particularly those men who were serving. A reader write-in to the army publication *YANK: The Army Weekly*, a magazine written for and by servicemen, exemplifies a common perception of Sinatra among American soldiers. Sgt. John H. Mader of Presque Isle, Maine, writes:

> Dear YANK:
> Say! Exactly why are men like Frank Sinatra and professional athletes like Leo Durocher and hosts of others classified 4-F for minor defects like a punctured eardrum? I am damn near blind, 20/800 in each eye, and I have seen poor GIs much worse off physically than I am. There is one guy here who has a glass eye and can't see very much out of the other. My buddies and I would like to know why athletes can't do the same nonstrenuous details half-blind men are asked to do?[35]

YANK provided the following answer:

> Most eardrums are perforated after infection has begun in the middle ear, and in the ordinary exposure of the field, to which even a limited-service soldier is subjected, the danger of reinfection is great. The Army says it doesn't want a lot of mastoid cases on its hands.[36]

Despite this relatively objective response, another reader followed up to say that they too had a "busted" eardrum yet somehow managed to enlist anyway.

---

[35] Sgt. John H. Mader, "Perforated Eardrums," *YANK: The Army Weekly*, February 11, 1944, 13. University of Washington Libraries' Special Collections.
[36] Mader, "Perforated Eardrums," 13.

Sinatra expressed in different media outlets during the 1940s that he wished he could have served,[37] but that did not prevent him from having to face rumors that he used bribes and his celebrity status to avoid active service throughout his career, rumors that were disproved only when FBI files related to Sinatra were released after his death in 1998.[38] And while other celebrities who did not actively serve (such as Bing Crosby) focused their creative output on patriotism-themed entertainment, Sinatra continued to sing primarily of love, romance, and heartbreak. This display of vulnerability proved to only increase the scrutiny directed toward Sinatra, because emotional strength was just as important to the image of American masculinity as physical strength.[39]

No doubt the public scrutiny Sinatra endured during World War II must have been challenging for the new star and likely contributed to the retooling of his image into a masculine, womanizing saloon singer in later decades (though these later years would see Sinatra face other challenges such as accusations of communist and mob associations). It is arguable, however, that the criticism Sinatra faced during the war years was slight compared to the torrent of accusations directed toward his young female fans.

A 1943 article in the *Chicago Daily Tribune* exemplifies the typical nature of press coverage surrounding Sinatra's teenage fans. The article recounts a scene at Sinatra's arrival in Pasadena, California:

A crowd of teen age girls stampeded in ecstasy today in greeting Tenor Frank Sinatra, idol of the nation's jitterbugs, upon his arrival here. Several of them fainted. They clawed and bit and pulled each other's hair. And they all screamed and shrieked as they fought on the station platform to get a closer view and the autograph of the boyishly earnest singer....

The girls in the back, deprived of a close view, began pushing and clawing. Then all semblance of order vanished. The frantic girls plunged thru tightly held police lines in an attempted bee line for their idol. They mauled and fell over each other in a melee that ranged all over the platform.[40]

---

[37] For example, the March 1944 issue of *Modern Screen* featured a photograph of Sinatra at the draft board before he received 4-F status that included the description, "At draft board, before he was 4-F'ed, Frank told press he hoped he'd be allowed to hang around for glimpse of new baby, thought he'd make a good soldier, wanted whack at OCS." Jean Kinkead, "Swoon Boy," *Modern Screen*, March 1944, 23.

[38] The FBI files indicate that Sinatra was correctly assigned 4-F status. Federal Bureau of Investigation, *Frank Sinatra*, C.F. Scatterday, March 30, 1960, https://vault.fbi.gov/Frank%20Sinatra/Frank%20Sinatra%20Part%206%20of%2030/view , accessed August 2, 2023.

[39] Savage, *Teenage*, 445.

[40] "Sinatra Is Saved from His Fans," *Chicago Daily Tribune*, August 12, 1943, 24.

Figure 1.6 *Swooner Crooner* (Warner Bros. Pictures, 1944).

The animalistic imagery in this review works to reveal what may have been society's biggest fear regarding the behavior of Sinatra's young fans: uncontrollable expressions of body and sexuality.

Looking back to Warner Bros.' 1944 short *Looney Tunes* film *Swooner Crooner*, we see this type of behavior represented in animated form. As described in the Introduction, the film portrays the "Flockheed Eggcraft Factory," managed by Porky Pig and staffed by dedicated hens, who lay eggs on a conveyor belt for the war effort. As the hens are working, they are distracted by a disembodied voice coming from outside, the source of which turns out to be a caricature rooster version of Frank Sinatra. The hens abandon their work and rush outside, no longer portrayed as devoted war workers, but hysterical fans who are wearing the bobby socks and saddle shoes associated with Sinatra's wartime teenage fans (Figure 1.6).

A panicked Porky Pig decides to take out a newspaper advertisement that reads, "Rooster Auditions! Singing Rooster Needed to Keep Hens Producing. Apply Porky Pig." The film then proceeds to show the auditions of various rooster portrayals of other popular male singers, including Nelson Eddy, Al Jolson, Jimmy Durante, and Cab Calloway.[41] None of these singers is suitable to Porky, who becomes discouraged until the rooster version of Bing Crosby appears, saying, "Now look it here, Porky old man. Let the old groaner take a whirl at those slick chicks." Rooster Bing Crosby then sings Cliff Friend's "When My Dream Boat Comes Home," and the swooning hens are revived. Rooster Crosby and rooster Sinatra then engage in a singing competition, which results in the hens laying enormous piles of eggs. Notably, a baby chick who has not even reached sexual maturity manages to lay an egg much larger than herself (Figure 1.7). Elated at all the eggs that have been laid, Porky asks the singers, "How did you ever make them lay all those eggs?" The roosters

---

[41] The portrayals of these singers in *Swooner Crooner* is addressed further in Chapter 3.

Figure 1.7 *Swooner Crooner* (Warner Bros. Pictures, 1944).

respond, "It's very simple, Porky. Like this," and sing a duet. Porky himself then proceeds to lay a pile of eggs.

As has already been discussed in this chapter, American teenage girls were under pressure to adhere to contradicting expectations regarding female roles and behavior alongside expectations to support the war effort in any way possible. Maintaining mainstream standards of feminine beauty, working in the public sphere only as a way to contribute to the war effort, and developing domestic skills and subdued behaviors was America's idea of an ideal woman. What society saw through media representation when it came to fans of Frank Sinatra, however, was the complete opposite of these characteristics. According to a significant portion of the media coverage surrounding Sinatra fans, teenage girls were unhinged. Images of screaming, fighting, and swooning girls plastered newspapers. Rather than contributing to the war effort, these girls were accused of having inappropriately misplaced priorities. To make matters worse in the eyes of American society, these girls were directing their inexcusable behavior toward the worst kind of male star: one that was scrawny, sentimental, and noticeably absent from military service.

This mindset is emphasized in the choice to illustrate Sinatra fandom using farm animals and their reproductive systems in *Swooner Crooner*, a film that was notably directed at children, and can easily be interpreted as a warning of the inappropriateness, and even danger, of young Americans devoting too much attention toward a popular icon in the midst of war.[42]

---

[42] *Swooner Crooner* is notably not the only time Sinatra was presented in cartoon form during the 1940s. The cartoon short *Little 'Tinker* (MGM, 1948) similarly portrayed a cartoon skunk version of Sinatra and his young fans as hysterical rabbits.

Before the hens hear Sinatra's voice, their sexuality is purely economic. Their egg laying is mechanical (literally performed on a factory conveyor belt) and there is no indication that this reproductive act has anything to do with sexuality or pleasure. Instead, eggs are laid only through a sense of duty. One hen, who is unable to produce an egg on her first try, looks ashamed at her failure and is forced to move back on the conveyor belt and try again. This part of *Swooner Crooner* proves to be a strikingly revealing depiction of the actual expectations surrounding female sexuality and behavior during World War II.

When Sinatra's voice enters, however, egg laying takes on completely different connotations. The hens lose all control over their reproductivity and laying eggs becomes effortless and emotional rather than forced and productive. Perhaps the few seconds of the film that are most indicative of stereotypes placed on Sinatra fans is the baby chick, which can be likened to a young teenager or even a child, who lays the biggest egg of all before she has even reached sexual maturity. It is clear that the creators of *Swooner Crooner* were tuned in to current media coverage and societal fears regarding how Sinatra's very human female fans were behaving.

Conclusion

A 1944 feature in *Time* magazine, which reads similarly to a nature documentary, serves as another example of how adult society viewed teenage girls as a distinctly separate social group. This viewpoint of course remains current today, as teenagers are seen as their own commercial market with their own cultural practices. During World War II, however, the distinction was more negatively pronounced, as difference from mainstream society usually suggested a lack of appropriate dedication to the war effort. Indeed, the *Time* magazine article, "Teen-Age Girls: They Live in a Wonderful World of Their Own," suggests this, indicating that "Some 6,000,000 U.S. teen-age girls live in a world all their own—a lovely, gay, enthusiastic, funny and blissful society almost untouched by the war. It is a world of sweaters and skirts and bobby sox and loafers, of hair worn long, of eye-glass rims painted red with nail polish, of high-school boys not yet gone to the war."[43] The article proceeds to lampoon the "capricious laws" of teenage girls and their mysterious slang.

---

[43] "Teen-Age Girls: They Live in a Wonderful World of Their Own," *Time*, December 11, 1944, 91.

Throughout, there is an emphasis on the idea that they are blissfully isolated from reality. According to the author, "In their social life teen-agers are primarily interested in themselves. High-school boys run a poor second and servicemen stationed near town are last. An old high-school boy home in uniform, however, is in a class by himself and rates tops."[44]

Naiveté, selfishness, hysteria. These were the characteristics American media saw in World War II teenage girls who demonstrated their adoration of Frank Sinatra in public. Throughout the following decades and even today, this is the narrative we still find in the national imagination regarding Sinatra's early career: questions of why these girls reacted this way to Sinatra specifically, what they gained from popular culture fandom in general as wartime Americans, and what the communities they formed around popular culture were really like remain noticeably absent. The next chapter dives into the social organizations teens developed and participated in—particularly Teen Canteens and fan clubs—and examines the unique cultural practices they created within these organizations. Contrary to public belief, these teens proved to be driven by a desire to develop professional skills, manage productive organizations, and foster feelings of autonomy within their lives.

---

[44] "Teen-Age Girls," 95.

2
Teenage Social Organizations

While World War II presented challenges for American youth who struggled to find clear purpose in the war effort in the midst of expanding opportunities for American adults, youth were also enjoying more freedom during the war years. Reasons for this were mixed, with some youth left with time on their own as a result of parents serving overseas or in the workforce in larger numbers. Although many young Americans spent their time productively, helping with household work, taking on part-time jobs or volunteer work, and socializing with peers in addition to attending school, this newfound independence led to increasing adult fears of juvenile delinquency.

Throughout the war years, newspaper headlines warned society of the dangers youth had the potential to instigate, with headlines such as "Gain in Juvenile Delinquency Exceeds Population Rise Rate"[1] and "Robber's Shots Go Wild. Both Prisoners Have Police Records, Starting with Juvenile Delinquency."[2] Fears regarding female sexual delinquency were especially rampant during World War II, and were in part fueled by the unrestrained displays of hysteria some young female fans showed toward Frank Sinatra, as noted in Chapter 1. One of the most infamous of these displays was what came to be known as the Columbus Day riot on October 12, 1944, when thousands of teenage girls overtook Times Square and the Paramount Theatre to see Sinatra, making national headlines for their unruly behavior and refusal to leave at the day's end.[3]

News coverage of juvenile delinquency was not completely unfounded in the 1940s. There were in fact reports of increased rates in criminal activity involving youth, which was attributed to a variety of factors including national tension and fear of war, more independence for youth, and the feelings of purposelessness many teenagers experienced during the war. And while

---

[1] "Gain in Juvenile Delinquency Exceeds Population Rise Rate," *Los Angeles Times*, December 24, 1942, 11.
[2] "Patrolman Foils Hold-Up, Seizes 2," *New York Times*, November 15, 1943, 21.
[3] For a more detailed description of the Columbus Day riot, see Jon Savage, *Teenage: The Prehistory of Youth Culture, 1875–1945* (London: Penguin Books, 2007), 442–443.

concerns regarding juvenile delinquency had been present in America throughout the first half of the twentieth century, the fear that juvenile delinquency might impede the war effort caused a renewed sense of alarm and call for action.[4]

Race also factored into assumptions regarding juvenile delinquency, not only because of the inherent racism already ingrained in American culture, but also because, as Lewis A. Erenberg notes, "Urban black youth faced more unemployment than their white peers and had fewer leisure outlets," and lived "in rooming houses apart from families more than other groups did."[5] This exasperated fears that unsupervised youth with no productive occupation would turn to delinquency.

The concern surrounding juvenile delinquency and how American youth were spending their time was not limited to parents and news coverage. The US government, in conjunction with local governments and community organizations, made an effort to provide youth with spaces and alternative ways to spend their free time in an attempt to keep them out of trouble. The most widespread of these attempts was the creation of a system of Teen Canteens (also called youth centers), organizations meant to provide recreational opportunities for teenage boys and girls in a way that felt safe and appropriately supervised to adults.

Although Teen Canteens were initially organized with the help of adult volunteers and chaperones and appeared to much of society to be places where youth primarily went to dance and listen to swing music, teenage members desired responsibility when it came to the management of their local centers. Far from showing reluctance to participate in organized recreation, which mass media defined as indicative of delinquency and promiscuity, American teens embraced their youth centers and demonstrated interest and proficiency in developing professional skills, managing fun and productive programming, creating opportunities to contribute to the war effort, engaging in the public sphere, and in some cases, encouraging racial and economic diversity within their communities.

Despite the success of Teen Canteens among both American boys and girls, many teenage girls sought out their own communities made up primarily of fellow girls. One way many American girls were able to find these communities was through war-era celebrity fan clubs. Like Teen Canteens,

---

[4] Grace Palladino, *Teenagers: An American History* (New York: Basic Books, 1996), 81.
[5] Lewis A. Erenberg, *Swingin' the Dream: Big Band Jazz and the Rebirth of American Culture* (Chicago: University of Chicago Press, 1998), 40.

fan clubs placed popular music and culture at the center of their organizations, yet this enjoyment of particular music, celebrities, and other cultural objects served as a springboard for teens to cultivate holistic experiences involving community building, career preparation, and contributing to the war effort and society at large.

Many war-era celebrity fan clubs included both male and female members. The membership of the expansive system of Frank Sinatra fan clubs during this time, however, was overwhelmingly teenage and female. While this is not necessarily surprising when considering Sinatra's primary fan base during World War II, the sheer number and management methods of these fan clubs lead to questions regarding why American teenage girls wished to be part of these types of communities and how their experiences in these groups differed from other youth organizations, such as Teen Canteens. Facing different challenges than teenage boys, specifically more uncertainty regarding their futures as women and different societal expectations surrounding gender roles and sexuality, Frank Sinatra fan clubs proved to provide teenage girls with spaces where they could use their shared love of the pop idol as a catalyst to navigate these challenges with understanding peers.

Beginning with an exploration into the structures and practices of World War II Teen Canteens, this chapter will then move to introduce the more intimate yet still expansive world of war-era celebrity fan clubs, particularly those dedicated to Frank Sinatra, providing a detailed reconstruction of how most clubs were organized and managed, typical member demographics, club publications, and the relationship between fan clubs and the entertainment industry. Driving this reconstruction are published club journals created entirely by club members. The cultures created within these clubs reveal that American teenage girls were given the opportunity to develop skills that would serve them in future work through club participation, such as writing, editing, and management skills. In addition, in an era defined in part by propaganda and consumer manipulation, fan clubs proved to demonstrate significant interest in cultivating power and engagement within the American entertainment industry, even if this power was, in many cases, imaginary.

Teen Canteens

Teen Canteens, also referred to as youth centers, were developed to provide safe, organized, and fun spaces American teens—both boys and girls—could spend time in. The idea was that if teens had a designated place to go, where they in fact wanted to go, they would be less tempted to cause trouble in public. The brainchild of Mark A. McCloskey of the Office of Community War Services, Teen Canteens were located in various community spaces, such as churches, schools, YMCA and YWCA rooms, and empty shops. Most were open afternoons and evenings, sometimes all week and sometimes only on weekends. Typical activities included listening to music on jukeboxes, dancing, games, crafts, and sports. Most Teen Canteens had themed decorations and a snack bar, the proceeds of which were used to support continued programming within the centers. In a 1945 report written by McCloskey on the success of Teen Canteens, a revealing document that will be worth quoting in length, it was noted that 1,700 of these youth centers were officially reported by recreation representatives, though McCloskey estimated that around 3,000 were actually up and running.[6]

While the initial motivation for starting Teen Canteen programs was based on concerns surrounding juvenile delinquency, McCloskey was notably observant in realizing that many American youth felt purposeless in the war effort. Most members of Teen Canteens were between the ages of fourteen and eighteen, making them too young for military service or full-time war work.[7] Teen Canteens could provide a way for youth to not only engage in recreation, but take on leadership roles and work as a group to contribute to the war. In the same 1945 report, McCloskey brings to light not only the creativity and resourcefulness of American youth in their Teen Canteens, but also their desire for purpose and how youth centers could help channel that:

> While we fought a war, the between-years boys and girls felt left out of the show. They didn't "belong." It was wanting to belong, to be important in something, to find a substitute for the "exciting things" their elders were doing, that set the stage for these youth centers....
>
> These young people converted old barns and garages, vacant stores or church basements into clubs of their own which rival many an adult nightclub. They introduced glamor into corners that were dull and drab, wielded paint brush with the uninhibited artistry of Surrealists, rehabilitated

---

[6] Mark A. McCloskey, *Youth Centers: An Appraisal and a Look Ahead . . . Based on Nationwide Survey*, report for Federal Security Agency, Office of Community War Services, Division of Recreation (Washington, DC: Federal Security Agency, 1945), 12.

[7] McCloskey, *Youth Centers*, 4.

furniture and equipment, even moved in on plumbing and lighting. As to names, only the imaginative young could conjure them: Hi-Teen; Swing-Inn; Jiving Jills and Jacks; Hep Kat Club; Eagles Nest; Jollywog Club; Hurricane Haven; Joy Teen; Shangri-La; Los Caballeros; Spider Web; Rhythm Rocker; Melody Mill; Harmony Hangout; Hubbub Room; White Hat Club; The Juke Box; Robins' Roost; Flamingo; Boogie Bar; Jive Hive.[8]

One of the primary reasons Teen Canteens were so successful among American youth was that they were organized and managed mainly by teen members themselves, although most all successful centers had at least one adult supervisor and were supported by local adult organizations. However, multiple sources indicate the importance of adult leaders maintaining an appropriate balance of support and unobtrusiveness. Teens benefited from adult advice and help, especially when first starting up a new center, but overall, teens wanted to feel like the centers were their own, not that they were being chaperoned like children. Having a sense of freedom and control was key to making sure teens would want to continue spending time in their centers. One 1944 report from the Associated Youth-Serving Organizations, Inc. reiterated the importance of subtlety in adult volunteers, noting, "It is of the utmost importance that this leadership be of the highest type—wise, unobtrusive leadership which will help advise and guide youth in its own planning and activities."[9] Teen members of these youth centers desired control not only in terms of the recreational aspects of Teen Canteens, but in maintaining finances and center rules as well. McCloskey wrote in detail about the achievements of teen members in these areas:

> Many of the centers have formalized and stabilized their organizations in written constitutions which set the objectives, give the qualifications for membership, list rules of behavior, and establish the responsibilities of the officers and committees, both youth and adult. These constitutions and by-laws are democratic statements of principles and procedures, formulated and adopted by the young people themselves.[10]

---

[8] McCloskey, *Youth Centers*, 2.
[9] Associated Youth-Serving Organizations, Inc., *On Teen-Age Canteens: A Memorandum*, October 1944, Oregon State Archives, sos.oregon.gov/archives.
[10] McCloskey, *Youth Centers*, 15–16.

In terms of funding Teen Canteens, teen members often managed themselves through collecting dues, proceeds from jukeboxes, concessions, and donations. In addition, members organized fundraising events like dances, talent shows, fashion shows, concerts, and bake sales.

Membership was also an important consideration for the youth leaders and members of Teen Canteens, many of whom not only proved to value socializing with peers from similar geographical and economic backgrounds, but also worked to make youth centers accessible to wider demographics. According to official reports, while some youth centers did not have very diverse memberships—particularly because most centers were geographically specific and catered to youth who came from similar neighborhoods—some centers did attempt to broaden their membership in a way that was more economically and socially inclusive. McCloskey reports:

> On the other side of the ledger are the many very real efforts to obtain a representative membership—efforts which show up the youth center in one of its most salutary aspects. One Ohio center, backed by approval of the community and the members, enrolled a number of youngsters who had been court cases....
>
> [T]welve centers [in Georgia] reported considerable membership from teenagers of underprivileged homes—frequently because a campaign had been carried on to recruit them. In a Columbus, Georgia, center, membership for those who cannot afford it is donated by interested citizens.
>
> In one agricultural community in Missouri, where there was little social mingling between land-owners and share-croppers, the youth center succeeded in getting young people from both groups to participate. It was an unprecedented development and a score for democracy.[11]

Despite the efforts of some Teen Canteens to diversify their membership, reports also existed of some centers suffering and even closing down because of disputes regarding race. Often, this was not due to discriminatory mindsets among teens themselves, but their parents, who were influenced by alarming media coverage of juvenile delinquency and danger, which was frequently connected with race. Many parents viewed Teen Canteens that limited participation to similar demographics within the same neighborhoods as a way to allow teens to safely interact with one another, without the risk

---

[11] McCloskey, *Youth Centers*, 4–5.

of mingling with teens deemed as unacceptably different from them.[12] As Grace Palladino notes, however, this mindset was becoming increasingly distasteful to many Americans who viewed segregation in America as no different from Nazi prejudices, "and teenagers were assigned the task of changing the nation's values" where their parents had failed.[13]

Teenage activism regarding racial and religious tolerance will be discussed further in Chapter 3, but it is worth noting in the context of Teen Canteens that many American youth were vocal in condemning their parents and older generations' attitudes of discrimination. One 1944 *New York Times* article, "As the Youngsters See Juvenile Delinquency," reflects these values among teens alongside their desire to take social change into their own hands. One excerpt from the article reads,

> When the question of vandalism and race prejudice was brought up the words "subversive influence" popped into the conversation. One lad pointed out that "the very fact that the form of vandalism is so similar in different sections of the country proves that it is definitely the result of an organized campaign to get hold of the youth of the country for a rotten thing."
>
> The boys and girls were almost unanimous in the belief that they themselves had no innate prejudices, that every instance of prejudice, intolerance and discrimination was due to adult influence either at home or in school, but mostly in the home.
>
> "It's perfectly natural," said a New York boy indignantly, "for a fellow to give another fellow a kick in the shins for some personal reason, but to beat up a boy just because he belongs to another racial or religious group is not a natural instinct. There are certain people in this country who want to destroy our democracy and they are trying to do it by arousing racial prejudices, just as Hitler did."[14]

As will be shown in Chapter 3, not all American youth desired to fight intolerance, and some continued to support practices of segregation, but there was a strong indication in both mass media and within youth organizations

---

[12] Palladino, *Teenagers*, 88–89.
[13] Palladino, *Teenagers*, 88–89.
[14] Dorothy Gordon, "As the Youngsters See Juvenile Delinquency: They Think Grown-ups Misjudge the Causes and Propose Some Measures of Their Own," *New York Times*, August 6, 1944, 16.

that many teens saw the fight against discrimination as one that they could take on more effectively than adults could.

While American youth felt adults were lacking in the realm of social justice, they did look up to adults in other ways. The careful preparation and management of finances, governance, and events that teen members demonstrated within their youth centers, alongside their efforts to consciously cultivate membership, undoubtedly served to help them build skills they could apply to future work in addition to providing them with a sense of purpose and structure during the war. This kind of professional development was important to teens, in part because they looked up to and hoped to emulate adults who were active in the armed forces and American workforce when they came of age. This interest in both honoring and imitating older Americans active in the war effort, particularly military personnel, was reflected not only in the professional ways teens managed their centers, but in the cultures they created within them.

The term "Teen Canteen" itself was borrowed from soldier canteens, where serving Americans could go to relax, socialize, eat and drink, and find distraction from their daily lives. While Teen Canteens were well organized and beneficial for American youth hoping to develop professional skills, the main draw was the same as that of soldier canteens—entertainment. The 1944 report from the Associated Youth-Serving Organizations, Inc. noted that "Youth likes to feel that it has a place similar to that of the soldier or sailor and with the same type of activities. Anything in the form of decoration or program that is like those in the servicemen's clubs will be helpful."[15]

As already noted, most Teen Canteens had a jukebox, and listening and dancing to music was top of the activity list in many centers. The same report describes the necessity for music and dancing for a successful youth center:

> Practically all of the centers have a juke box. This also can be a source of good revenue for center maintenance. It provides the everyday music for dancing. Occasionally, some of the centers hire orchestras by means of a special charge for a particular occasion or revenues earned from the juke box. There can be no objection to occasionally hiring an orchestra.[16]

---

[15] Associated Youth-Serving Organizations, *On Teen-Age Canteens*, 5.
[16] Associated Youth-Serving Organizations, *On Teen-Age Canteens*, 5.

In an era when teen dating and socializing between different genders was often at the forefront of both youth and adult minds—though in different ways—Teen Canteens served as an effective compromise between teens who craved this kind of socialization and independence and parents and adult leaders who were fearful of this socializing moving too far. And although Teen Canteens played an important role in the lives of many wartime youth, American teenage girls in particular benefited from cultivating communities that mainly consisted of other girls. Like Teen Canteens, these communities were often built with popular music and culture at the center. For one of the most condemned and criticized groups of American teenage girls during the war—the devoted fans of Frank Sinatra—these communities were paramount in helping them develop purpose, confidence, and professional skill sets, all while adoring their favorite pop idol away from the public eye.

Organized Adoration: Purpose and Professionalism in Frank Sinatra Fan Clubs

Dear Frances,

I read in the Sept. issue of Band Leaders where you and your friends were organizing a Frank Sinatra fan club. I would like very much to join it....

I have been a Sinatra fan since 1943, and I always will be one. I am strictly a Sinatra fan.

You might like to know how old I am so I'll tell you. I am 16 years old and a Senior in High School.

I am waiting to hear from you and I hope it will be soon.

Sinatrally yours,

Laura Paul[17]

Dear Frances,

I am very much interested in your Frank Sinatra fan club. Mr. Sinatra is really tops on my list of favorites. I think he is more than something to scream and swoon over. I would like very much to join your club and

---

[17] Laura Paul to Frances Bergstrom, August 7, 1945, Sinatra-ana Collection, Hoboken Historical Museum, Hoboken, NJ (hereafter cited as Sinatra-ana).

to help you form it. I'm twelve years old and hope I'm not too young to be a member. . . .
Very, very sincerely,
Beth Hurwitz[18]

In various entertainment publications in 1945, including the September issue of *Band Leaders* magazine, it was announced that Frances Bergstrom of Minneapolis, Minnesota, was forming a new Frank Sinatra fan club and seeking members. Bergstrom asked candidates to send her a letter indicating their interest, which she would return with more information and a questionnaire to answer about themselves, their interests in popular singers, and their own musical experience. The result was a wealth of correspondence from prospective members throughout the United States, primarily teenage girls.

Bergstrom's was one of many American celebrity fan clubs during the 1940s. These clubs made up an extensive network of communities that provided American teenage girls with safe spaces to express themselves and connect with like-minded peers as they navigated the many challenges facing young women during the war. In Frank Sinatra fan clubs specifically, the opportunity to connect with fellow fans while simultaneously being able to autonomously manage their own organizations served as refreshing relief from the continuous public scrutiny and challenges these particular female fans—and some male fans, as will be addressed in Chapter 4—faced from society at large. The remainder of this chapter will delve into club publications and member demographics, their organizational practices, and examine the notably present and productive relationship these fan clubs fostered with the entertainment industry as a whole.

Fan Club Journals

The heart of most 1940s celebrity fan clubs was the club journal. For many clubs that had members located throughout the United States, who likely would not have met each other in person or would only meet those members in their local chapters, the club journal was the lifeblood of a club's identity. In many ways, club journals could serve as an equalizer for

---

[18] Beth Hurwitz to Frances Bergstrom, c. August 1945, Sinatra-ana. Used with permission of the author.

groups of American youth who came from various economic and cultural backgrounds. Members could generally submit journal material at any level of anonymity they desired, and because members often never met in person due to geographical distance and other factors, club journals could provide opportunities for girls who may have faced prejudice or felt out of place in their schools or communities to become involved with a different group of supportive peers.

Most clubs could not obtain "official" status with their respective celebrities and certain commercial fan club organizations, as will be discussed further on, without a journal. The club journal was the single most important connecting force in most clubs where fans could share information, and more significantly their creative contributions, in a way that was accessible to all members. Just having a journal, however, was usually not enough for most clubs. For those clubs that wished to exhibit professionalism in their fan activities (which was most of them), journals had to maintain certain quality standards. For example, the June 1941 issue of *El Club Cabana*, published by the Fan Club League (a large club devoted not to one particular star, but to celebrity fan clubs in general), included advice from member Mary Munger on maintaining quality in club journals. This feature, titled "A Few Rules for Editing a Paper," listed certain basics that most fan clubs followed in their journals:

1. *Don't* sacrifice quality for quantity. In other words, don't use cheap stencils which give poor copies. Nothing is more detrimental to enjoyable reading of a fan club news than peering into each line trying to read the print. Rather have a few clear-cut pages than many that aren't readable.
2. *Do* date your issues—either with the month or season.
3. *Do* have a list of the officers, honoraries, etc., near the front, preferably on the index page if you have one—not stuck off someplace in the back.[19]

Most fan club journals followed these basic formatting practices in order to create a structured foundation for presenting member content that included everything from music and film reviews to original poetry, as will be explored throughout the remainder of this study.

---

[19] Mary Munger, "A Few Rules for Editing a Paper," El Club Cabana (June 1941), 15, Hal Mohr & Evelyn Venable papers, Margaret Herrick Library, Academy of Motion Picture Arts and Sciences, Beverly Hills, CA.

An increasing number of scholars have begun to focus on fan-made texts, particularly "fanzines," as primary sources for analyzing popular culture and audience relationships. This scholarship has thus far tended to focus on media fandom and fan texts from about the 1970s on, with a particular focus on science fiction and media fandom.[20] Some authors, such as Henry Jenkins and Mark Duffett, have contributed influential texts that include broader discussions of fanzines and how these objects reflect fan practices more generally.[21] Duffett provides a particularly helpful definition of fanzines and how they shaped fan communities, describing them as "a place in which fans could socialize and express their own creativity" with close relationships between editors and readers. Duffett also highlights less censorship as a feature of fanzines, noting content can "vary in terms of public acceptability from family-friendly newsletter to twisted commentaries bordering on obscenity."[22] Jenkins also defines fanzines in part by the relationship between writer/publisher and reader, noting that feedback and distribution of publications generally happens directly between the author and reader, creating a more intimate relationship than readers can experience with professionally published media and fan magazines.[23]

The club journals produced by 1940s celebrity fan clubs certainly align with the characteristics Duffett and Jenkins use to identify fanzines. Club members, for instance, sent submissions and suggestions directly to the editors and were free to express opinions they may not have been comfortable expressing in other areas of their lives. There were some distinctive features of these clubs and their journals, however, that distinguish them from other fan communities often discussed in scholarship. These included an emphasis on soliciting journal material from as many club members as possible, as opposed to journal content being the responsibility of only a small group of individuals, and pursuing relationships with large commercial entertainment organizations.

---

[20] Examples include Teal Triggs, *Fanzines: The DIY Revolution* (San Francisco: Chronicle Books, 2010); The Subcultures Network, *Ripped, Torn and Cut: Pop, Politics and Punk Fanzines from 1976* (Manchester: Manchester University Press, 2018); and Paula Guerra and Pedor Quintela, eds., *Punk, Fanzines and DIY Cultures in a Global World: Fast, Furious and Xerox* (Cham, Switzerland: Palgrave Macmillan, 2020).

[21] Henry Jenkins, *Textual Poachers: Television Fans and Participatory Culture* (New York: Routledge, 2013); Mark Duffett, *Understanding Fandom: An Introduction to the Study of Media Fan Culture* (New York: Bloomsbury Academic, 2013).

[22] Duffett, *Understanding Fandom*, 185.

[23] Jenkins, *Textual Poachers*, 159.

Turning to Frank Sinatra fan clubs specifically, we can see these practices clearly reflected in club journals, in turn providing extremely intimate insight into the lives of American teenage girls, how they interacted with popular culture, how they managed their clubs, and the role the entertainment industry played in shaping club mentalities.

Frank Sinatra Fan Club Membership Procedures and Demographics

As was highlighted in Chapter 1, a very specific image of the typical World War II–era Frank Sinatra fan existed in American imaginations and media. That image was of a teenage girl who wore bobby socks and saddle shoes and neglected her responsibilities to family, school, and country in the name of devoting all of her attention to Frank Sinatra. When in the presence of Sinatra, this girl lost sight of any maturity or self-control she may have possessed and transformed into an animalistic creature that shrieked and fainted upon hearing Sinatra's voice.

It would be incorrect to say that the development of this image was totally unfounded. Many teenage fans of Sinatra did in fact publicly respond to Sinatra in physical and emotional ways that shocked a nation that strove to define itself during World War II by reserved yet unshakeable strength and morality. What mass media and the public generally did not see, however, were the ways in which thousands of these teenage girls pursued their fandom for Sinatra and other stars in ways that were privately and publicly productive. This is not to say that many fans did not exhibit both characteristics in their fan practices. Instead, the published journals of fan clubs reveal that there were many different ways and levels at which teenage girls could express their adoration toward their favorite celebrities.

Sinatra fan club journals reveal that most club members were females between the ages of thirteen and eighteen. Almost all journals included sections that featured information about individual members such as age, hometown, and hobbies as a way to narrow the often large geographical gap between members. Often labeled "thumbnail sketches," these profiles further solidify the authority of club journals as windows into the experiences of teenage girls during this particular moment in American history. For example, one thumbnail sketch in the Spring 1945 journal of the Society for

Souls Suffering from Sinatritis, the *BowTie Bugle*, introduces member Judith Newman of Cleveland Heights, Ohio:

> Judy is the Vice President of the Cleveland Chapter of the "Society" and an ardent of "our boy." She is nearly eighteen and admits, to her chagrin, that she does'nt [sic] look a day over twelve. Brown-eyed Judy is almost 5', and weighs 98 pounds. She has brown hair, and a great big grin. Judy's favorite pastime, when not listening to Frank, is to go to at least two different movies in one day, but eating comes a close second. She is a senior at Heights High School, and at the moment hasn't any particular career in mind. Guess she just hopes to meet "that certain one" soon.[24]

The September 1945 issue of *The T-Jacket Journal*, produced by the Sing with the Sinatras Club, features member Helen Reid of Atlanta, Georgia:

> [Helen] is secretary of our club and is a very cute blonde. She attends Girls High in Atlanta and has been an ardent admirer of Frank's since 1942. She is 5'6" tall and has a wonderful personallity [sic]. She adores Cornell Wilde [sic] and Gregory Peck (can you blame her?). She has two good looking cousins in the navy and some cousins and uncles in the army. Helen is fiftheen [sic] and looks seventeen. Her favorites in music are Chopin and she loves to attend movies. Take my word for it she is well worth knowing.[25]

Member profiles throughout Sinatra fan club journals followed a similar format and included varying levels of detail. Some, like the above, included information about physical characteristics, families, hobbies, and experiences surrounding Frank Sinatra. Others offered less specific information, listing only names, ages, and maybe hobbies or a note about why they liked Sinatra. Members were generally free to offer up as much or as little information about themselves as they desired. As will be discussed in Chapter 3, club journals provide clues that Sinatra fan club membership in particular may have represented some diversity in terms of racial and ethnic backgrounds and economic classes, but on the surface, club journals allowed

---

[24] "Thumb-Nail Sketches," the Society for Souls Suffering from Sinatritis, *BowTie Bugle*, no. 7 (Spring 1945), 7, Sinatra-ana.
[25] "Thumbnail Sketches," Sing with the Sinatras Club, *The T-Jacket Journal* (September 1945), 5, Stuart A. Rose Manuscript, Archives, and Rare Book Library, Emory University, Atlanta, GA (hereafter cited as Rose MARBL).

members to participate with one another on what felt like an equal and relatively anonymous level. Rather than participating together in a physical space where appearances, accents, or other characteristics may have affected member's opinions of each other, whether consciously or unconsciously, club journals instead created the illusion that members were all similar to one another because of their love of Sinatra. Devotion to Sinatra and age were generally the only characteristics a potential member was truly required to possess to join most clubs, and in many cases were the only characteristics fellow members knew about each other.

This criterion for Frank Sinatra fan club membership is demonstrated through membership application procedures, which usually consisted of sending a letter to the club president, filling out an informational card, or a combination of both. Looking again to Frances Bergstrom, whose Frank Sinatra fan club was announced in the September 1945 issue of *Band Leaders* magazine, we see that membership qualification for her club was based primarily on genuine interest in Sinatra and music in general. In one letter to a prospective member, Bergstrom also indicates the age requirement for membership was between ten and twenty years old.[26] After a hopeful member wrote to Bergstrom to express their interest, she would send them a questionnaire to fill out. Aside from asking for their birthdate and address, all of the questions pertained to their interest in popular musicians, their own musicianship, and their interest in helping with club duties. Figure 2.1 shows an application questionnaire filled out by member Gloria Campen, who was fourteen at the time of her application. At the end of the questionnaire, Campen offers her suggestion for what to name the new club.

Bergstrom's application procedure was more involved than most other clubs, which often only required a person's name, address, and dues to join. The Ora e Sempre Sinatra (Now and Always Sinatra) club relied mostly on current member references to recruit new members and indicated that "All new members names and dues" should be sent to one of the club administrators. In this case, a formal letter was not even required for membership.[27]

While initially it may seem that member anonymity would limit the connection these fans could feel with one another, it in fact allowed them the

---

[26] Frances Bergstrom to Beth Hurwitz, August 1, 1945, Sinatra-ana.
[27] Ora e Sempre Sinatra Club, *Ora e Sempre Sinatra*, Edition I (c. Summer 1945), 11, author's collection.

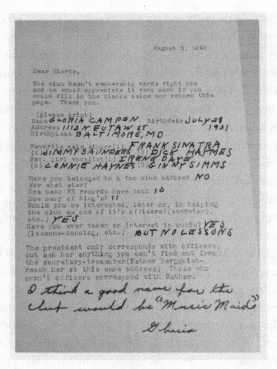

Figure 2.1 Application questionnaire for Gloria Campen from Frances Bergstrom (August 3, 1945). Hoboken Historical Museum.

freedom to define their relationships exclusively through common interests rather than social or economic positions. This perceived equality also allowed members to work together to efficiently run their clubs, in turn providing them with chances to develop professional skills they may not have otherwise had the opportunity to pursue as young Americans.

Fan Club Structures and Business Practices

In 1946, a book about Frank Sinatra's then short career was published, titled *The Voice: The Story of an American Phenomenon*. Written by a longtime writer for the *New Yorker*, E. J. Kahn Jr., this book was a compilation of various articles Kahn researched and wrote about Sinatra's wartime success. Kahn indicated that he had personally met Sinatra on a number of occasions, but that much of his information came from people who worked for Sinatra, including his press agent, George Evans. In reference to Sinatra's fan following, Kahn wrote:

> According to George Evans ... there are forty million Sinatra fans in the United States. Evans estimates that there are two thousand fan clubs, with an average membership of two hundred, and he has further estimated (by means of logarithms and a press agent's intuition) that only one per cent of the Sinatra fans have yet bothered to join a club.[28]

These numbers and Evans supposed "logarithm" were likely exaggerated, as one may expect from a celebrity publicity agent, but it is clear that there were a large number of Sinatra and other celebrity fan clubs in existence during World War II and the years immediately following. Evidence of clubs dedicated to all of the biggest 1940s celebrities can be found throughout various commercial entertainment publications of the era, especially in lists published in movie and fan magazines.

An article written by legendary gossip columnist Hedda Hopper in the September 1945 issue of *Modern Screen* provides one such list of Frank Sinatra fan clubs specifically, highlighting the creative and sometimes comical names fans came up with for their clubs. Included on this list was The Frank Sinatra Solid Sending Swooning Screaming Sirens, Grand Guy Frank Club, The Swoonettes, The Bobby Sox Brigade, The Hotra Sinatra Club, The Semper Sinatra Swoonettes, The Fascinated Fans of Frankie, The Frank Sinatra Swoon Club, and The Sigh Guy Club.[29] Kahn provides another list of notable names in his book, including Subjects of the Sultan of Swoon, The Bow-tie-dolizers, Frankie's United Swooners, and the Our Swoon Prince Frankie Fan Club.[30]

Clubs that managed to gain advertising space in fan and entertainment magazines often received significant numbers of inquiries from prospective members, as was the case with Frances Bergstrom's club. But even for those clubs that operated on a smaller scale, it was still imperative that clubs maintain a certain level of professionalism and business savvy to ensure their clubs would function successfully. Unknown to much of mainstream society,

---

[28] E. J. Kahn Jr., *The Voice: The Story of an American Phenomenon* (New York: Harper & Brothers, 1946), 43.
[29] Hedda Hopper, "Join a Fan Club!," *Modern Screen* (September 1945), 108.
[30] Kahn, *The Voice*, 75–76.

which tended to believe that very little went into fan club participation aside from listening to music and gushing over stars—Kahn claimed that Sinatra club meetings "amount to little more than convening around a phonograph or radio and listening to The Voice"[31]—teenage girls were developing professional skills through their fandom that could contribute to future jobs and other opportunities.

The history of American women during World War II privileges the stories of women who joined the workforce, armed forces, and took up other important roles previously closed to them, but very little attention has been given to those who were too young to engage in such employment. American women were not allowed to enlist in areas of the armed forces such as the WAVES (Women Accepted for Volunteer Emergency Service) until they were twenty (boys could enlist at eighteen)[32] or take on industrial work until they were eighteen,[33] but many younger teenage girls still desired to find occupation during the war that felt productive and purposeful.

Many also hoped to find employment as soon as they were old enough and sought ways to prepare. Fan club participation proved to offer valuable experience for teenage girls in which they could develop skills such as organization and money management, writing, editing, and publishing. While most observers of fan culture did not see or acknowledge this aspect of fandom, some commercial institutions did. For example, in the same *Modern Screen* article by Hedda Hopper that lists Sinatra club names, Hopper acknowledged the business-like nature of fan clubs, writing:

> Fan clubs are really a business. Files must be kept, bank accounts coped with, hundreds of letters sent out. People who don't know about fan clubs are apt to think of them as a dozen or so kids sitting around cutting out pictures of their favorite movie star. They do that too, but believe me, that's only a minor item. The amount of time, money and energy that goes into these clubs gives me gray hairs just thinking about it.[34]

In the same article, Al Delacorte, the executive director of *Modern Screen*, contributed his opinion that suggested fan club participation could lead

---

[31] Kahn, *The Voice*, 75–76.
[32] Doris Weatherford, *American Women and World War II* (Edison, NJ: Castle Books, 2008), 39.
[33] Weatherford, *American Women and World War II*, 121.
[34] Hedda Hopper, "Join a Fan Club!," 113. Originally cited in Katie Beisel Hollenbach, "Teenage Agency and Popular Music Reception in World War II–Era Frank Sinatra Fan Clubs," *Journal of Popular Music Studies* 31, no. 4 (Winter 2019): 108.

to exciting careers in the entertainment industry, mentioning Sinatra fans specifically:

> Join. Pay that nickel [for dues]. Relax. And your life starts looking up. Fan clubs are fun—if fun's what you want.
> But if your sights are set on the future, that nickel pays even greater dividends. No high school business or journalism course can teach you the practical knowledge you pick up working for a club. You'll learn to write. You'll learn publicity. You'll learn to handle money. And I'm talking from experience. Most of our staff are former fan-clubbers. We've come to insist on it. Modern Screen is duck soup for kids like that. They speak the language. Modern Screen's just another club journal to them—only bigger.
> As for publicity, just ask Frankie [Sinatra] Boy's manager, George Evans. Ask him what proportion of his staff has had fan club experience. You'll die when he tells you!
> So you see, fan clubs are fun—nothing but fun, if that's the way you want it. But for kids with ambition, they are Route One to success in the fields of journalism and publicity. And all for a nickel![35]

While Delacorte emphasizes journalism and publicity as possible careers that evolve from fan club participation, the skills members cultivated could be applied to a variety of different jobs.

Most celebrity fan clubs adhered to a standard organizational structure. There was almost always a club president or two co-presidents, supported by various other roles such as vice president, secretary, journal editor, and treasurer. As in any business, these administrators had to manage various essential roles to keep their clubs afloat, including maintaining member lists and addresses, distributing journals on time, and perhaps most important, collecting dues. Most issues of celebrity fan club journals included a reminder to members to send in their dues to ensure their club's survival. An especially firm example can be found in the inaugural journal of the Ora e Sempre Sinatra club:

> Please try to be prompt in paying your dues each month. You've no idea how expensive it is to run a club, and if two or three people are late in paying their dues it makes a great difference. We are asking that dues be in

---

[35] Hopper, "Join a Fan Club!," 113.

by the fifteenth of every month. The first month you fail to pay you will be notified, but will receive that month's offer (snaps, etc.); the second month a notice but not the offer; the third month the last and final notice; and then if we haven't heard from you by the fourth month you will be dropped from the club. If you wish to prevent any mix-up perhaps you'd like to pay dues several months in advance. This is easier for us as well as you. We're sorry we have to be so severe, but things can't be run smoothly unless we have this prompt payment. If you think this too unfair write Nonie and perhaps some other agreement can be made.[36]

Notices about dues generally emphasized that money was used not only to maintain essential tasks, but to improve club practices and experiences for all members. Juanita Stephens, president of the Sing with the Sinatras Club, asked members to consider contributing extra money in addition to their dues in order to purchase a mimeograph machine in the September 1945 issue of their journal, the *T-Jacket Journal*. Stephens emphasized the purchase would help to improve the quality and efficiency of their club journal, reflecting a common goal among clubs to create professional-looking publications:

I've felt like I've been letting the members, the club and Frank down these past three months. We haven't had the paper out because of the paper shortage and because I couldn't find a way to get the paper printed. Finally I scouted around and found out where we could buy a memographing [sic] machine. Although it took more money than we had in the treasury, I took what we had and added to it and made a down payment. Now we must pay $5 a month for the next three months. Believe me if it was possible to do otherwise I would not ask for contributions to help pay for it, but it was so expensive. So if you care to, will you please contribute something. With the help of this machine the Journal will come out regularly and it will be much better, neater and larger.[37]

Club journals accounted for most of the administrative efforts within clubs, alongside membership tracking and recruitment. Clubs hoped to consistently increase membership in order to cultivate more submissions for

---

[36] Ora e Sempre Sinatra Club, *Ora e Sempre Sinatra*, Edition I (c. Summer 1945), 11, author's collection.

[37] Juanita Stephens, *T-Jacket Journal* (September 1945), 1, Rose MARBL.

journals, achieve rankings in commercial fan club contests, and generally to welcome more fans to their communities.

Emphasis on member growth is apparent in club journals both in solicitations for journal submissions and notices of membership contests. The June–July 1946 issue of the *T-Jacket Journal* includes information about a membership recruitment contest, indicating that "To girls recruiting most new members in months August, Sept., October, will go prize of any 3 Sinatra records. Send prospective members' addresses to us, we'll get in touch with them."[38] The first issue of the *Voices Echo*, produced by the Our Guy Frankie Fan Club, highlights the importance of having as many members as possible submit material for the club journal:

> We do want our magazine to be one of the best, don't we members? So let's work and work hard. Send in all the poems and stories to me. Tell about any thrilling moment you have spent with Frank and let us feel that we were there with you enjoying that breathless moment with "OUR GUY." So as I said before friends let's work hard because it's well worth it.[39]

Quality of journals and increasing membership were important not only for the enjoyment of current members, but also for recognition among commercial fan organizations, which were generally associated with movie and radio fan magazines. The relationships that clubs pursued with these commercial organizations reflected the belief of many young fans that they held power within the entertainment industry, and that it was important to express their opinions, desires, and criticisms to commercial powers in order to influence popular culture content. Whether this power was real, imaginary, or a combination of both has been a continuous topic of study, but it is clear that fans viewed themselves as essential influences in the trajectory of American popular culture.

Club Relationships with and Power in the Entertainment Industry

Commercially published Hollywood and radio fan magazines of the 1940s were the products of an enormous network of advertising and star creation

---

[38] Sing with the Sinatras Club, *T-Jacket Journal* (June–July 1946), 1, Rose MARBL.
[39] Loretta (last name unknown), "Letter from the Secretary," *Voices Echo* 1, Issue 1 (May 1945): 1, Sinatra-ana.

that was largely directed toward the wallets of American women and girls. While movies and radio shows of course drew both male and female audiences, fan magazines had promoted the idea that enthusiastic fans were a distinctly feminine image decades before World War II. This was in part a result of growing unease over representations of American masculinity in the first decades of the twentieth century.

Fueled by such historical moments as Theodore Roosevelt's encouragement of a "strenuous life," World War I, and the Great Depression, demonstrations of male emotional vulnerability and frivolity were increasingly discouraged in American society.[40] In the entertainment industry, this attitude led to a shift in catering to both men and women as ardent movie and star fans, to directing marketing attention primarily to women. As Kathryn H. Fuller explained in her study of movie fans, *At the Picture Show: Small-Town Audiences and the Creation of Movie Fan Culture*, fan magazines began to shift to a more gendered focus starting in the late 1910s, and "as the image of the frivolous female fan magazine reader took hold, it became much harder for popular culture to imagine male movie fans or the possibility of their interest in movie magazines or movie fan culture."[41]

By the time the United States entered World War II, the idea of movie and celebrity fan culture being dominated by females was fully established, and fan magazines of the 1940s were quite obviously created with women in mind. Magazines such as *Modern Screen*, *Photoplay*, *Screenland*, and *Radio Mirror* included numerous ads for women's clothing, hygiene, and beauty products, and advice columns directed toward young, and primarily white, women and girls.[42] Notably, these magazines also included extensive invitations for readers to engage directly with them, fostering the idea that fans had influence in entertainment publications and the industry as a whole.

It is no secret that the entertainment industry has from its beginnings been fueled by a complex network of harnessing star and advertising power for commercial gain. The relationship between the industry and its

---

[40] For more on the development of American masculine standards, see Gail Bederman, *Manliness & Civilization: A Cultural History of Gender and Race in the United States, 1880–1917* (Chicago: University of Chicago Press, 1995); Allision McCracken, *Real Men Don't Sing: Crooning in American Culture* (Durham, NC: Duke University Press, 2015); and Christina S. Jarvis, *The Male Body at War: American Masculinity during World War II* (DeKalb: Northern Illinois University Press, 2010).

[41] Kathryn H. Fuller, *At the Picture Show: Small-Town Audiences and the Creation of Movie Fan Culture* (Washington, DC: Smithsonian Institution Press, 1996), 145–148.

[42] See the Introduction for more discussion on representation in fan magazines.

consumers, and the question of whether or not these consumers hold any power within the industry, has encouraged fruitful scholarship over the past decades. For example, Miriam Hansen's influential study of early film spectatorship suggests that any power American fans felt they had in the star system was largely imagined and carefully constructed by entertainment companies themselves, and the "very arbitrariness of the cinematic marketplace, the element of chance in the 'discovery' of a star, became part of that promotional discourse, essential to the myth that the star was a creation of his or her loving public."[43] In fan magazines specifically, it is true that these publications created their own devices for audience participation primarily for their own monetary gain, but as the decades progressed into the 1940s, it became clear that reader participation portions of most fan magazines were essential to the magazine's success.

A single issue of a popular fan magazine usually provided multiple opportunities for readers to actively participate in the magazine's content, with encouragement to contribute opinion letters, sign up for fan clubs, or send their addresses to receive special material. For example, the October 1944 issue of *Screenland* included information in their regular column, "Fan's Forum," about submitting opinion letters in order to "let the stars know how you like them and their pictures," offering cash prizes for the best letters.[44] The same issue also includes multiple calls for original poetry from music publishing companies and opportunities for readers to send their addresses in order to receive celebrity photographs. *Movie Stars Parade* magazine included a regular feature, "Betty Burr's Original Fan Club Corner," that provided tips for clubs to improve their membership and journals and encouraged them to write to the magazine.

Providing opportunities for readers to interact with magazines became vital for publications working to compete in the growing fan magazine industry, which Marsha Orgeron notes "intended to transform spectators *of* celebrity culture into participators *in* celebrity culture."[45] And while Hansen is correct to indicate that much of American fan participation was facilitated by commercial entities, the increasing interactions between fan magazines and fan-made clubs especially demonstrate how fans succeeded in publicly

---

[43] Miriam Hansen, *Babel and Babylon: Spectatorship in American Silent Film* (Cambridge, MA: Harvard University Press, 1991), 248.
[44] "Fan's Forum," *Screenland* (October 1944), 12.
[45] Marsha Orgeron, "'You Are Invited to Participate': Interactive Fandom in the Age of the Movie Magazine," *Journal of Film & Video* 61, no. 3 (Fall 2009): 4.

inserting themselves into the American entertainment industry, whether or not their opinions were truly considered.

Looking to how Frank Sinatra fan clubs in particular interacted with commercial fan organizations from the perspectives of club members, we can see that clubs took their relationships with these organizations very seriously and encouraged as many members as possible to contact fan magazines on Sinatra's behalf. This viewpoint contrasts with other fan cultures in history, such as the Riot Grrrl movement, which was strongly anti–mass media and desired to distance itself from commercial media and publications.[46] Sinatra fan club journals, on the other hand, make clear that members truly believed their efforts in submitting opinions to commercial fan magazines and boosting Sinatra made a difference in his potential success. Using *Modern Screen* magazine and its own fan organization, the Modern Screen Fan Club Association, as a case study reveals the persistence of Sinatra fans in supporting their idol and the close relationship clubs felt they shared with the organization.

The main purpose of the Modern Screen Fan Club Association (MSFCA) was to encourage fan clubs to demonstrate high levels of organization, membership, and productivity, particularly in their club journals. Most issues of *Modern Screen* magazine and many other fan magazines included pages with lists of fan clubs readers could join if they had interest, but the MSFCA took this encouragement to participate in club culture a step further by offering prizes and status for the best clubs. Founded in 1944, the MSFCA's initial purpose was to connect readers with fan clubs. One of the earliest mentions of the organization appears in the November 1944 issue toward the bottom of a page advertising different reader write-in opportunities. The short feature, headlined "How to Join a Fan Club," reads:

> Have yourself a time! Join one or more of the 60 fan clubs we've listed and get snaps of your favorite stars, club journals, chance for pen pals—even meet the stars themselves! Read about the new MODERN SCREEN Fan Club Association. Free, send a LARGE, self-addressed, stamped (3c) envelope.[47]

---

[46] Despite this mindset, Joanne Gottlieb and Gayle Wald note how some commercial media publications, particularly *Sassy* magazine, attempted to work in the Riot Grrrl movement's favor. See Joanne Gottlieb and Gayle Wald, "Smells Like Teen Spirit: Riot Grrrls, Revolution and Women in Independent Rock," in *Microphone Fiends: Youth Music & Youth Culture*, ed. Andrew Ross and Tricia Rose (New York: Routledge, 1994), 250–274.

[47] "How to Join a Fan Club," *Modern Screen* (November 1944), 26.

By 1946 and 1947, the MSFCA had grown in popularity and gained a more prominent position in the magazine. The January 1947 issue included an entire feature article devoted to the MSFCA—which had previously been part of a regular newsletter available only to members of the association—that praised club participation and encouraged more to join. The article, which was named after the newsletter the MSFCA previously only sent to members, *The Fans*, provides a description of the MSFCA, benefits of joining, and information about club contests. One section of the article describes the MSFCA in more detail and notably boasts a membership of 500 clubs, compared to sixty in 1944:

> Without a doubt, the MSFCA is the only organization of its kind in existence. You know, of course, that *Modern Screen* was the first magazine to get behind fan clubs one hundred per cent and put all of its vast resources at the disposal of fan clubbers. Each MSFCA club—and there are nearly 500—is an independent, authorized group. And that word, "authorized," is very important! No club is admitted to membership unless the star whom it honors *recognizes* and *approves* its existence. So you can be sure that belonging to an MSFCA club is something special, and that you'll have the full cooperation of your star![48]

Until this article appeared in 1947, the magazine itself did not provide many details to readers about what exactly was expected of clubs that joined the MSFCA and benefits of membership, reserving that information for designated members. The journals of Frank Sinatra fan clubs, however, reveal with exciting clarity what it meant for a club to be a member of the MSFCA.

One indication of the enthusiasm most Sinatra fan clubs held toward the MSFCA can be found in the June–July 1946 issue of the *T-Jacket Journal*, produced by the Sing with the Sinatras Club. The issue includes a feature encouraging members to continue producing content for the club in order to compete in the MSFCA's latest club contest:

> All of you are or will be receiving the MSFCA's paper, "the FANS." It tells you all the news, so we're just urging you on. A new Trophy cup contest is starting. Help our club win that cup for our league. Let's do win that

---

[48] Shirley Frohlich, "The Fans," *Modern Screen* (January 1947), 22, 100.

cup! Keep sending in snaps and write more for the journal. It all counts! Common' Singers, let's win that cup! What say, hey?[49]

The Summer 1945 issue of *Sinatra-ly Yours*, produced by the Semper Sinatra's Fan Club, provides more specific information regarding club participation in the MSFCA. Club member Marijane Hardin of Bellflower, California, wrote to her fellow members reminding them that they would all need to work together if they were to reach their goal of making it to the Modern Screen Fan Club Association's top five league. Hardin explains how clubs were rated by the MSFCA using a point system and provides criteria from the MSFCA on how clubs can earn points. Hardin writes:

> First thing I want to receive in my little ivy covered mailbox (honest) is a letter from each Club Chapter prexy, listing the names and addresses of all her members. Without that I'm like Frank without Nancy, so pleeeze help me. Make it soon too, huh?
> The requirements for points given in the MSFCA are for the following:
> 1. Fan-Fun Contest (best article or poem)
> 2. Most worthwhile club activity
> 3. Candid-Camera Contest
> 4. Contribution to war effort
> 5. Most active correspondent
> 6. Best journal
> 7. Cooperation with MSFCA
> 8. Greatest increase in members

From that you can readily see how easy it is to make points if we really try. So I'll be waiting to hear from all the prexys—and then we'll really make Frank proud of us.[50]

These guidelines, which initially did not appear in *Modern Screen* magazine but in their newsletter, *The Fans*, which was sent to MSFCA members as described above, make clear that fan club recognition within the MSFCA went far beyond simply registering a club name with them. Clubs were expected to work hard to earn mentions in the magazine, which in turn

---

[49] Sing with the Sinatras Club, "Modern Screen Fan Club Association" (June–July 1946), 5, Rose MARBL.

[50] Marijane Hardin, "Chapters," *Sinatra-ly Yours* (Summer 1945), 7, Sinatra-ana.

provided clubs with publicity for membership growth. Clubs were motivated to participate not only because they wanted new members, but also because, as Hardin's guidelines suggest, there was a belief that by growing a club to reach "official" status with an organization like the MSFCA and the celebrity a club was dedicated to, they were somehow directly connected with the stars they admired and could be noticed by them.

In general, celebrity fan clubs could only claim "official" status if they wrote to and received permission to form from the celebrity in question. Of course, this usually meant receiving permission via a star or studio's employee, but nonetheless, official status was paramount for most clubs to feel they were legitimate. Some publications even refused to print news from clubs that could not provide proof of their official status.[51] Clubs that received official status were very proud of doing so. Most club journals of official clubs listed at the top of each journal the various associations and/or official statuses they were associated with. In addition, after achieving official status, many clubs wrote to celebrities and other public figures to ask that they consider becoming honorary members of their clubs, which could act as another mark of legitimacy and was usually indicated at the top of club journals alongside other achievements.

While association with public figures and organizations like the MSFCA was generally considered the ultimate mark of a club's success, fan club engagement with the entertainment industry went beyond seeking out these accolades. Almost all celebrity fan clubs truly believed they had a responsibility to vocally support their stars in order to help them gain further fame and opportunities within the industry. A feature in the April–June 1943 issue of *Nelson Eddy Notes*, published by the Nelson Eddy Club, for example, includes some of the letters members had sent to fan magazines on Eddy's behalf in an effort to encourage more members to do the same. An excerpt from one letter to *Photoplay* magazine from member Marianne Jesse, who believed Eddy should be given more roles in films, reads:

> It seems a crime that one with Mr. Eddy's accomplishments should not be given the opportunities he deserves. Concert sell-outs, year after year, prove that he has a huge following. Now, if the motion picture producers

---

[51] Samantha Barbas, *Movie Crazy: Fans, Stars, and the Cult of Celebrity* (New York: Palgrave, 2001), 123.

would only realize this and give Mr. Eddy a real chance, I'm positive he'd be "top box office" because we'd [(his fans)] put him there!⁵²

The May 1945 issue of the Our Guy Frankie Can Club's journal, the *Voices Echo*, provided mailing addresses for the editors of *Modern Screen*, *Movie Stars Parade*, and *Movieland* magazines so members could write to them on Sinatra's behalf, explaining:

> The purpose of this column is for all the members to write to the people listed below and ask for articles, stories, and pictures of Frank to appear in their magazines. Send only a postcard and watch the results. Please mention the club though. After the article appears write a note of thanks. . . . I would like all the members to write to: Max Factor, 1666 North Highland Ave., Hollywood, California and thank them for sponsoring the new Frank Sinatra Show.⁵³

Similarly, the Fall 1944 issue of *Sinatra-ly Yours*, produced by the Semper Sinatra's Fan Club, reminds members: "Don't forget to keep writing Frank at his studio and also asking movie mags to print stories about him. We want to keep Frank on the top now that he is there. Requests are what makes a star, so don't forget to keep requesting. Mention this club tho."⁵⁴

In addition to writing to magazines, members were encouraged to contact radio stations to promote Sinatra, and especially vote in contests that stations often hosted between Sinatra and Bing Crosby. Recognizing the enormous fan base of both Sinatra and Crosby, radio stations frequently hosted what were called "Battle of the Baritones" to increase listener numbers. Listeners would hear both singers perform over a set period of time then vote for their favorite. The September 1944 issue of the Slaves of Sinatra's journal, *The Voice*, notifies members of one such contest:

> Elsie Ellovich tells us that there's a contest in the East being conducted by station W.I.N.S. between our boy and Bingo. So far, Frank's 120,000 ahead of the Groaner and has tolled over 2,000,000 votes BUT there's a possibility

---

⁵² Marianne Jesse, letter to *Photoplay* magazine, published in *Nelson Eddy Notes* (April–June 1943), 13, Paul Henreid papers, Margaret Herrick Library, Academy of Motion Picture Arts and Sciences, Beverly Hills, CA.
⁵³ Our Guy Frankie Fan Club, "Postal Patrol," *Voices Echo* 1, Issue 1 (May 1945): 1, Sinatra-ana.
⁵⁴ Semper Sinatra's Fan Club, *Sinatra-ly Yours* 1, no. 3 (Fall 1944), 7, Sinatra-ana.

that Bing may win yet (gruesome thot) so send in your vote right away to . . . Battle of the Baritones, Station W.I.N.S., New York City. Just write Frank's name on a post card and sign your name and address. It's very important that you remember this latter detail. Only one vote to a person. Get that vote in right away![55]

Ensuring that Sinatra won as many of these contests as possible was important to his fan clubs, and keeping each other notified of these types of events helped to cultivate the sense of community participation and industry influence that was key to the fan club experience.

Conclusion

As was discussed in Chapter 1, American teenage girls faced challenges in finding place and purpose during the chaotic years of World War II. But as celebrity fan club journals demonstrate, participating in fan clubs and interacting with the entertainment industry in structured ways proved to be one way that girls could use their fandom to feel that they had influence in war-era popular culture, which for many was of the utmost importance for maintaining wartime morale. This chapter has focused on the ways fan club participation provided members with practical experiences, such as management, budgeting, and writing and editing, which could help them prepare for potential future working roles. The next chapter will delve into the ways Sinatra fans brought their fandom into the public sphere as a way to engage with important issues such as racial and religious tolerance and international relations.

[55] Slaves of Sinatra, "Notice," *The Voice* 1, no. 3 (September 1944): 1, Sinatra-ana.

3

Finding "the Voice"

Organized Fandom as Political Platform

Gary, Ind.—Sinatra sang while Gary's race-haters burned.

In a heart-to-heart talk with 5,000 stomping, screaming adorers, Frank Sinatra told the teen-agers to "kick out" the adult instigators of this town's bitter anti-Negro high school strike.

While enraged leaders of Froebel high school's race hate drive pleaded with students to ignore Sinatra, the famous crooner led his converts in a pledge to fight racism....

Fresh, eager and with less than an hour to catch his plane, the singer led the cheering students in a pledge of "allegiance to the democratic ideals in our home, schools, in our independent youth organizations."
—"Frank Sinatra Fails to Break Gary Hate Strike,"
Chicago Defender, November 10, 1945

In September 1945, a group of white students walked out of Froebel High School in Gary, Indiana in protest of the school's integration of previously segregated classrooms. Although there had been a population of black students at the school since the mid-1910s, these students were placed in classrooms separate from those of white students and were restricted from participating in most of the extracurricular activities the school offered. In the 1940s, a new principal was instated at Froebel High School, Richard Nuzum. Recognizing the shifts in cultural and social paradigms within America during the immediate aftermath of World War II, Nuzum attempted to bring change to Froebel High School through initiatives such as creating a biracial parent-teacher association, integrating the swimming pool, and allowing black students to participate in extracurricular activities such as music.

These efforts resulted in backlash from some of the school's white students and their parents, who believed the school should remain segregated, and accused Nuzum of showing preferential treatment to the black student population. According to the *Indianapolis Recorder*, the striking students presented demands to the school board, which included "'kicking out' the Negro students from Froebel, the discharge of Principal R. A. Nazum [sic] and the 'ending of biracial experiments' at the high school."[1] The school board denied these demands, and the strike persisted throughout the fall, gaining national media attention.

As the strikes continued, community leaders and organizations searched for ways to end the conflict and convince students to return to school. It was announced that in early November, Frank Sinatra would travel to Gary in order to preach a message of tolerance to students in the hope that the singer's popularity would work to convince striking students to return to school. In the end, Sinatra's appearance did not do much to resolve the strikes, and they continued through November. However, the fact that a popular icon who during the war years was ridiculed by much of adult society for his appearance, lack of military service, and displays of vulnerability was called in at this moment to aid in a social emergency is worth taking a second look at.

The national response to the so-called hate strikes in Gary was largely condemnation toward those who were outwardly attempting to suppress the rights of black Americans immediately after the United States spent nearly four years fighting to defeat different forms of racism and fascism in World War II. In this immediate postwar context, Sinatra was praised by media outlets for his efforts in speaking to America's youth about democracy—one article in the *Chicago Defender* described him as "a true American"[2]—and he would go on to receive an Honorary Academy Award in 1946 for his work in the 1945 short film *The House I Live In*, which served as a platform for Sinatra to discuss racial and religious tolerance.

Although Sinatra gained recognition for speaking out about racial and religious tolerance during the war years and beyond, the way he influenced his teenage fans in this regard and how they adopted a similar mindset during World War II has been overlooked. This chapter will examine how young Sinatra fans during the 1940s used their fandom as a platform to champion and discuss social issues including racial and religious tolerance, liberal

---

[1] "Students' Walkout Mixed in Race Hate," *Indianapolis Recorder*, September 29, 1945, 1.
[2] "Frank Sinatra—A True American," *Chicago Defender*, December 1, 1945, 12.

political beliefs, patriotism, and international cooperation, using Sinatra as a focal point for these discussions. Beginning this examination will be a look into Sinatra's experience and identity as an Italian American and how this identity influenced his reception and audience base. What we ultimately find in Sinatra fans' writings are communities of teenage girls who were using their fan groups to seriously talk about important issues of the day without facing condescension from adults and others who did not find value in the opinions of America's female youth.

Sinatra and Italian American Identity

On September 28, 1944, one year before the start of the Froebel High School strikes, Frank Sinatra was invited to have tea at the White House with President Franklin D. Roosevelt. Press coverage of the event mostly focused on the casual conversations the two public figures supposedly shared, including a discussion of Sinatra's talent in making girls swoon. One account of the meeting in the *Los Angeles Times* provided minimal details, indicating the visit was not one of great political significance:

> Sinatra had little to say after the tea. The President didn't ask him to sing.
> "He kidded me about the art of how to make girls faint," Sinatra said.
> "And Frank swooned himself," put in [Rags] Ragland. "We had to pick him off the floor twice."
> "Why are you a fourth-term supporter?" a reporter asked Sinatra.
> "Well," thoughtfully replied the Voice, "you might say I'm in favor of it."[3]

Sinatra's alleged comradery with FDR and his support of a fourth-term reelection was in fact very significant, however, as this was an early example of Sinatra's lifelong involvement in politics and other social issues. More significantly during the 1940s, Sinatra's outspoken support of liberal political figures and values influenced a large portion the country's female youth, whose voices and opinions generally fell near the bottom of the nation's priority list.

To understand Sinatra's political and social beliefs and why they were important to his fans, we must look at Sinatra's own experiences as an Italian

---

[3] "Sinatra Explains to President Art of Making Girls Swoon," *Los Angeles Times*, September 29, 1944, 6.

American citizen growing up in New Jersey during the early decades of the twentieth century. Sinatra's family was part of a group of Italian immigrants who, from the start of their mass migration to the United States in the late nineteenth century, faced prejudice from other Americans.[4] This prejudice stemmed largely from American perceptions of Italian religion, criminal culture, and geography. In *The Routledge History of Italian Americans*, Richard N. Juliani describes how Catholic Italian Americans not only faced new language and economic barriers in the United States but also struggled to find acceptance in a largely Protestant nation. Catholicism in America was already a relatively underrepresented religion, and the addition of Italian immigrants was viewed as a further blow to the position of Catholic Americans, who in general did not view ethnic diversity in their religious group as a positive attribute.[5]

Other factors affecting American perceptions of Italian immigrants included ideas regarding race and Italian geography. American mindsets, media, and official written documents such as the Dillingham Commission's Report on Immigration fueled the idea that there were certain levels of "whiteness" in America and Europe, and that not all levels were equal.

Yet again, Warner Bros. Pictures' 1944 short *Swooner Crooner* serves as a brief but telling example of how American society viewed Sinatra's celebrity persona and the behavior of his young fans, as well as how race and ethnicity influenced the nation's perceptions of Sinatra's effect on American teenage girls. As we will remember, Porky Pig panics at the sudden halt in his hens' egg production from the disruption of Rooster Sinatra's performance. To get things back on track, Porky lists a newspaper advertisement soliciting "Rooster Auditions! Singing Rooster Needed to Keep Hens Producing. Apply Porky Pig." The film then shows a string of auditions performed by racially caricatured rooster versions of other male singers of the era, including Jimmy Durante, Nelson Eddy, Al Jolson, and Cab Calloway.

In *Swooner Crooner*, the largely white, working hens (with a small number of brown hens) in the film are not revived by a performance of the minstrel song "Shortnin' Bread" by a brown rooster whose voice resembles Nelson

---

[4] A portion of this examination of Sinatra's experience as an Italian American and his fans reception of this identity originated in Katie Beisel Hollenbach, "Teenage Agency and Popular Music Reception in World War II–Era Frank Sinatra Fan Clubs," *Journal of Popular Music Studies* 31, no. 4 (Winter 2019): 149–151.

[5] Richard N. Juliani, "Italian Americans and Their Religious Experience," in *The Routledge History of Italian Americans*, ed. William J. Connell and Stanislao G. Pugliese (New York: Routledge, 2018), 193–194.

Eddy's, a performance of "September in the Rain" by a brown Al Jolson rooster with white gloves and painted white mouth, reflecting Jolson's fame as a blackface performer, a brown Jimmy Durante rooster, or a black Cab Calloway rooster. This brief scene succinctly demonstrates the incredibly complex system of race relations in the United States during World War II in cartoon form. Not only was a black performer deemed unfit for the hens, but neither were performers who held similarly ambiguous levels of whiteness as Sinatra, in the case of Jimmy Durante, also Italian American, and Al Jolson, a Jewish immigrant. Only when Bing Crosby—a male performer cherished in the 1940s for his portrayal of mainstream values of American whiteness, strength, and patriotism—appears are the hens able to get back to their war work, even more efficiently than before.

On a government level, this notion of ambiguous and geographically specific whiteness was reflected in the Dillingham Commission's Report, published in 1911. According to the report, Southern and Eastern European immigrants were inclined to have a harder time assimilating in America and were more involved in criminal activity than Northern and Western Europeans. The report demonstrated the prevalent behavior of early twentieth-century Americans, which unfortunately continues to this day, to equate certain physical characteristics with certain moral and intellectual characteristics.[6] This idea was applied within individual countries as well, and in the American mindset, immigrants from the south of Italy were deemed more racially inferior than northern Italians. Frank Sinatra, whose father was from Sicily, endured insults and suspicion born from these rooted beliefs in American society throughout his life.

When Italy declared war on the United States on December 11, 1941, shortly after the Japanese attack on Pearl Harbor, Italian Americans faced dangerous public suspicion as Japanese Americans did. The US government assigned unnaturalized Italian immigrants "enemy alien" status and some were sent to internment camps.[7] Many Italian Americans experienced the challenge of feeling genuine patriotism as Americans and a desire to aid America's war effort while simultaneously worrying about friends and relatives they had in Italy and maintaining a sense of pride and love toward

---

[6] Matthew Frye Jacobson, *Whiteness of a Different Color: European Immigrants and the Alchemy of Race* (Cambridge, MA: Harvard University Press, 1999), 78–82; and Peter G. Vellon, "Italian Americans and Race During the Era of Mass Immigration," in *The Routledge History of Italian Americans*, 214.

[7] Stefano Luconi, "Contested Loyalties: World War II and Italian-Americans' Ethnic Identity," *Italian Americana* 30, no. 3 (Summer 2012): 151–167.

their homeland. Some Italian Americans navigated this by volunteering for military service in the Pacific to fight the Japanese, in turn avoiding having to fight directly against Italians, while others served as cultural aides between the United States and Italy.[8]

The status of Italian Americans also strongly influenced the political campaign of Franklin D. Roosevelt. Many Italian Americans resented Roosevelt's condemnation of Italy and felt the president did not distinguish between the people and culture of their homeland and the specific fight against fascism at hand.[9] As a result, Roosevelt had to work to attract Italian American voters during his wartime campaign, in part by garnering support from prominent figures of Italian descent such as Fiorella La Guardia and Frank Sinatra.[10]

Influenced by all of these intertwining factors in the lives of Italian Americans throughout the first half of the twentieth century, Sinatra used his celebrity status in the 1940s as a platform for speaking on public issues including racial and religious tolerance and juvenile delinquency. He was open in speaking about the bullying he faced as a child due to his Italian heritage and presented himself as coming from a working-class background (though his family did relatively well financially), which allowed him to build seemingly personal and relatable connections with his fans, especially those who may have come from similar backgrounds and faced similar prejudice. For American youth from marginalized communities, and especially Italian Americans, Sinatra served as one of the first examples of an Italian American who achieved public success and fame, alongside other figures such as Joe DiMaggio and Fiorello La Guardia. One quote in the *Manchester Guardian* suggests that even in Britain, observers were recognizing the sense of class identification fans shared with Sinatra, whether or not fans were really "children of the poor" as the author suggests:

> Although I am told that devotion to The Voice is found in all classes of society, nearly all of the bobby-soxers whom I saw at the Paramount gave every appearance of being children of the poor. Oddly enough, this fragile young singer has, among other qualities, a sense of strength and power: there is a solidarity and sureness about him that are out of all proportion to his physical frailness. I would guess that these children find in

---

[8] Matteo Pretelli, "Hollywood's Depiction of Italian American Servicemen during the Italian Campaign of World War II," *European Journal of American Studies* 15, no. 2 (Summer 2020): 4.

[9] Luconi, "Contested Loyalties," 159.

[10] Luconi, "Contested Loyalties," 161.

him, for all his youthfulness, something of a father image. And beyond that, he represents a dream of what they themselves might conceivably do or become. He earns a million a year, and yet he talks their language; he is just a kid from Hoboken who got the breaks. In everything he says and does he aligns himself with the youngsters and against the adult world. It is always "we" and never "you."[11]

Journalist Pete Hamill suggests that Sinatra, along with other Italian American public icons, "changed forever the way Americans saw Italian Americans. For the first time, Americans with other ethnic origins wanted to be like these children of the Italian migration. And their accomplishments changed the way Italian Americans saw themselves."[12] Sinatra's rise to fame, influence on America's youth, and public speaking in support of liberal politics are what landed him an invitation to visit FDR at the White House, not the fact that he made girls swoon.

Sinatra's most well-known project in terms of his activism efforts during the 1940s is the 1945 RKO Radio Pictures short film *The House I Live In*, which included and was named after the 1942 song of the same title. The ten-minute-long film shows Sinatra encountering a group of boys outside a recording studio who are bullying another boy because his religion is different from theirs. Sinatra confronts them, saying they must be Nazis if religion is the reason they do not like the other boy. The boys protest that they are certainly not Nazis and in fact have fathers who fought against Nazis during the war. Sinatra proceeds to explain to them that Americans of different races and religions all aided in the war effort, and that religion should make no difference to anyone, unless they are "a Nazi or somebody that's stupid." Sinatra then sings the title song, and the boys leave as friends with their former bullying victim.

The film received an Honorary Academy Award in 1946 and was championed by Sinatra's fans, many of whom printed the film's dialogue in full in their fan club newsletters. While the film focuses primarily on religious tolerance, Sinatra also spoke out against racial discrimination throughout his life, as did his fans during the 1940s. It is important to note, however, that not all minorities received Sinatra's support in equal measure during

---

[11] "The Voice and the Girls: Mr. Frank Sinatra's Pedestal," *Manchester Guardian*, January 10, 1945, 4.
[12] Pete Hamill, *Why Sinatra Matters* (Boston: Little, Brown, 1998), 119.

the war. It is true that Sinatra made good efforts in speaking in support of European ethnic minorities, such as his own Italian American family, as well as African Americans. Again, for American youth who identified themselves in these ways, the fact that Sinatra spoke in support of them created a welcoming space for a more diverse fan community than in those of other stars. Finding these types of diverse communities was not easy during World War II. While the United States felt strongly that it was combating intolerance by fighting Hitler, the reality was continued discrimination at home, especially toward African Americans. In the military, for example, despite the need for manpower and the willingness of many African Americans to serve, African Americans were initially barred from serving in the US Air Corps and Marine Corps. They were allowed in the Army, Navy, and Coast Guard but were placed in segregated units and mostly assigned roles as laborers.[13] In the midst of this kind of discrimination, Sinatra fans wrote in support of a more racially tolerant society in their club journals, as we will see, yet there was one group that was generally absent from these narratives, Japanese Americans.

As Sinatra speaks to the boys in *The House I Live In* about the importance of tolerance and diversity in America, he does so using the example of different kinds of Americans working together to fight the Japanese, referring to them as "Japs." This attitude stemmed from a nationwide shift in the portrayal of the Japanese in America after the 1941 attack on Pearl Harbor. As Christina S. Jarvis explains, the US government felt the need to "reinvent" the Japanese in the American mindset in order to "explain early U.S. losses in the Pacific and to provide an appropriate foe for America's fighting manhood."[14] While German soldiers were certainly vilified in American media, they at least tended to be portrayed as humans (although Hitler himself was often caricatured as an animal). The Japanese, on the other hand, including soldiers and civilians, were portrayed as "subhuman or animalistic."[15] This image was so widespread in the American imagination that it did not seem out of place for Sinatra to attack the Japanese and therefore isolate Japanese Americans in a film dedicated to preaching acceptance. Although Sinatra may have cultivated a more diverse fan following than some other stars and

---

[13] Joe William Trotter Jr., "From a Raw Deal to a New Deal? 1929–1945," in *To Make Our World Anew*, Vol. 2: *A History of African Americans since 1880*, ed. Robin D. G. Kelley and Earl Lewis (New York: Oxford University Press, 2000), 160.

[14] Christina S. Jarvis, *The Male Body at War: American Masculinity during World War II* (DeKalb: Northern Illinois University Press, 2010), 124.

[15] Jarvis, *Male Body at War*, 128.

made efforts to use his star status as a tool for promoting social change, we can unfortunately assume that the combination of mass incarceration and racism toward Japanese Americans meant they likely did not have access to what otherwise felt like an accessible fan community.

The rest of this chapter will examine the ways in which Sinatra's teenage fans used their fan communities to explore ideas surrounding diversity, politics, and values in America and internationally, which proved to demonstrate a much higher level of maturity and social responsibility than society usually gave them credit for. However, it is important to remember when viewing this fan activity that, just as there are today, there were still groups of Americans who were excluded from what was a seemingly open-minded group of popular culture participants.

Fan Writings on Tolerance

As noted in Chapter 2, the average age of Sinatra fan club members is relatively easy to determine, as ages were usually listed in member profiles of fan club journals. Determining class and racial demographics is more difficult, because these characteristics were generally not listed in club journals. Other components of fan club journals, fan support of Sinatra's social and political ideals, and Sinatra's cross-class image of both a sophisticated singer and "regular" guy from a working-class background, however, suggest that Sinatra had the potential to appeal to a relatively diverse audience. In addition, the ability to remain fairly anonymous within fan clubs contributed to the feeling of equality among club members. As Janice L. Booker writes, "Being a Sinatra fan as a bobby soxer offered the chance to affiliate with girls unlike themselves, crossing social lines, economic classes, ethnic differences, and school cliques."[16] And the consistency with which Sinatra fan club members participated in their clubs and interacted with each other in club journals demonstrates that these somewhat invisible friendships felt real. Even if members never met in person due to geographical distance or other factors, it is clear that members felt their club journals were valuable tools in creating genuine relationships with one another and promoting diversity and tolerance both in and outside of their clubs.

---

[16] Janice L. Booker, "Why the Bobby Soxers?," in *Frank Sinatra: History, Identity, and Italian American Culture*, ed. Stanislao G. Pugliese (New York: Palgrave Macmillan, 2004), 77.

The April–May 1946 issue of the *T-Jacket Journal*, published by the Sing with the Sinatras Club, reprinted a quote from Sinatra found in the March 1946 issue of *The Fans*, the fan club newsletter distributed by the Modern Screen Fan Club Association. Sinatra reportedly submitted the following call to action to his fans:

> Although there are no exact figures available, it is pretty safe to estimate that there are millions of young people who are members of fan clubs. What a tremendous force and influence you could be if your efforts and energies were directed toward combatting that black plague of bigotry and intolerance that now threatens the free institutions and the happiness of the peoples of the world.[17]

Members of Frank Sinatra fan clubs did not really need Sinatra to publish this encouragement in *The Fans*. As soon as Sinatra began publicly speaking about his political ideals and issues of racial and religious tolerance, his fans began discussing these same issues within their club communities, especially when the release of *The House I Live In* was announced. Most club journals included at least an announcement of the film and a brief description, such as that found in the seventh edition of the *BowTie Bugle*, published by the Society for Souls Suffering from Sinatritis club:

> Frank Sinatra will star in a short film for RKO, the theme of which is racial and religious tolerance, called "The House I Live In." Directed by Mervyn Le Roy and produced by Frank Ross, the film will devote all proceeds to a charity leading in Juvenile activity. Sinatra began and finished the film the week before he left on his overseas entertainment tour.[18]

Similarly, the first edition of the Ora e Sempre Sinatra Fan Club's journal reported on the upcoming release of *The House I Live In*, noting the film's release would hopefully prompt an active response from fans:

> We're all waiting for [Sinatra's] picture, "The House I Live In," a short subject picture made about tolerance. If you have kept up on his articles in the

---

[17] Frank Sinatra, *The Fans* (March 1946), quoted in *T-Jacket Journal* (April–May 1946), 13, Stuart A. Rose Manuscript, Archives, and Rare Book Library, Emory University, Atlanta, GA (hereafter cited as Rose MARBL).

[18] The Society for Souls Suffering from Sinatritis, *BowTie Bugle*, no. 7 (Spring 1945): 6, Sinatra-ana Collection, Hoboken Historical Museum, Hoboken, NJ (hereafter cited as Sinatra-ana).

movie mags., etc., you know the great work he has been doing. We hope soon there will be a way for his fans to help in the campaign for racial and religious tolerance.[19]

Once the film was released, many clubs published the film's script in full in their journals. Whether or not it was their primary goal in doing so, this proved to be one way to make the film's message accessible to all club members, even if they could not attend the film in a theater.

Especially after the release of *The House I Live In*, Sinatra fan clubs began creating their own ways to discuss the issues Sinatra addresses in the film. The Sing with the Sinatras club, for example, implemented a regular feature in their journal, the *T-Jacket Journal*, which they called the "Tolerance Page." Club members were encouraged to submit essays, poems, or other creative expressions of their views on tolerance. The February–March 1946 issue of the journal advertised a contest for the best contribution to the "Tolerance Page," which emphasized the importance of aiding Sinatra in his activism. The instructions for the contest indicated the theme was "Tolerance, Democracy and Us," and encouraged members that "Frank's doing so much in fighting racil and religeous [sic] intolerance, that the least we can do is to help him" (Figure 3.1). Club president Juanita Stephens included her own contribution later on in the issue to express her views on tolerance using an algebraic equation (Figure 3.2). Club members already knew Stephens enjoyed algebra from her member profile in an earlier issue of the journal.

Beth Hurwitz, member of the Frank Sinatra Music Club, contributed a short essay to the club's June 1946 journal titled "Why I Like Frank Sinatra," which included a short mention about his activism efforts: "Another thing that I like about 'The Voice' is that he goes to schools and makes speeches about how wrong it is to be intolerant of someone's race or religion."[20] Based on other correspondence between Hurwitz and the club's president, Frances Bergstrom, Hurwitz was either twelve or thirteen years old when she wrote the essay.

Another letter to Frances Bergstrom from Cecilia M. Kelty includes a lengthy essay—which was likely meant as a submission for the club journal—on Kelty's views regarding tolerance and Sinatra's activism. The essay, titled "I Want to Talk to You about Frank," begins, "I want to talk to

---

[19] "We Hear," *Ora e Sempre Sinatra*, Edition 1 (c. Summer 1945), 3, author's collection.
[20] Beth Hurwitz, "Why I Like Frank Sinatra," *Sinatra Scope* (June 1946), 9, Sinatra-ana. Used with permission of the author.

> **************
> TOLERANCE ESSAY CONTEST NEWS.
> "So many Gods, so many creeds,
> So many paths that wind and wind,
> Yet just the art of being kind,
> Is all this sad world needs."
>
> With this quotation, "the House I live In," and Frank as inspiration I want to tell you the new contest, the rules and the object.
> 1st. Frank's doing so much in fighting racial and religeous intolerance, thatthe least we can do isto help him.
> 2nd. The prizes will be warded to the Best essay andthe 2 runneruppers-- The Best will be printed,The other 2 quoted in part.
> 3rd. The subject is "Tolerance,Democracy and Us".or onthat effect.
> 4th- Rules:a The contest will last from March 12--July12th.
> b. The essays should be over 50 words and under 200 words.
> c. Send them to Juanita Stphens. d. Judges to be announced later.
> e. winner to be annoucne in August issue and prizes awarded.
> Go to it fans, I know you have ideas on thesubject and I kn ow thatyou cando anything you want to. I waiting!
> **************

Figure 3.1 "Tolerance Essay Contest News," *T-Jacket Journal* (February–March 1946), 7. Rose MARBL.

> ***************
> "Algebra"
> How do you like algebra? I think its fun. You can think of an algebra problem in so many ways. In veiw of one of America's greatest problems lets think of ;   x   equals   Races,religions
>   z   "   Peace and Happiness
>   y   "   fighting and hate
>   a   "   Americans
> Which shall it be?   x and a = z
>   or   x and a = y
> You see, Americans and all people of all races must work live together, and help each other if the algebra is to equal "z".
> You'll say what has this to do to me. It has a lot to do with you, and you and yes, you. We are all future citizens.Our country will be what the people are and the world will be what America will help to make it.
> What about it, Are we going to let down the thousands of boys who've fought and even died for our peace and happiness? I have a feeling you'll all say no. So lets declare the second equation x and a equals y worng, and lets then work the 1st equation x and a equals z and know something, hey--its right!!
> **************

Figure 3.2 "Algebra," *T-Jacket Journal* (February–March 1946), 11. Rose MARBL.

you about Frank Sinatra. Not about Frank Sinatra, the guy with the terrific voice, but about Frank Sinatra, the guy who is doing all in his power to help stop juvenile delinquency, fighting as hard as he can for equality and tolerance."[21]

While discussions of race relations within Frank Sinatra fan clubs did not necessarily lead to extreme action or change—to use Ruth Frankenberg's work, some of these girls may have been "much more sharply aware of racial *oppression* shaping Black experience than of race *privilege* in [their] own life," thus "conceptualizing [their] own life as racially neutral"[22]—it is significant that these teenagers were cultivating their own ideas about these issues using a popular icon as a springboard. These discussions within their club communities would influence how teenage girls continued to develop their individual identities as wartime and postwar citizens, in turn influencing how the nation would approach these same social issues in the future. Similarly, Sinatra fan clubs provided a space where teenage girls could begin shaping their own political values outside of the influence of their parents and teachers.

Although many Sinatra fans were too young to vote—the voting age in the 1940s was twenty-one—the combination of an increasing emphasis on patriotism in American society and Sinatra's own political ideals encouraged young fans to take an active role in supporting the war effort, and more specifically, Franklin D. Roosevelt. Many fan club journals included material reminding members to support the war by purchasing war bonds and stamps, and tributes to FDR appeared relatively frequently, especially after his death in 1945.

War bonds especially were a popular topic within Sinatra fan clubs and American youth in general, as they were a tangible way young people could support the war effort. In Sinatra fan club journals, reminders to purchase war bonds and stamps were often included at the end of introductory letters from club presidents or announcement pages. These reminders became a kind of standard signature, indicating how prominent war bond programs were in daily American life. The end of the announcements page in the first edition of *Ora e Sempre Sinatra*, for example, published by the Ora e Sempre Sinatra club, reads, "This about covers it for this time. But remember keep

---

[21] Cecilia M. Kelty to Frances Bergstrom, c. 1945, Sinatra-ana.
[22] Ruth Frankenberg, *White Women, Race Matters: The Social Construction of Whiteness* (Minneapolis: University of Minnesota Press, 1993), 49.

buying those victory bonds and stamps."[23] A letter from the club secretary in the fall 1944 issue of *Sinatra-ly Yours* concludes, "Once again may I remind you all to write me—please. Keep boasting Frankie—and buy War Bonds 'til Victory."[24] Many clubs went a step further and held their own war bond raffles. The co-presidents of the Society for Souls Suffering from Sinatritis informed club members in the seventh edition of their journal, the *BowTie Bugle*:

> We are going to have a raffle. We will raffle of [*sic*] a $25 war bond. We want ALL of you to help in the selling of the tickets. If we do not notify you to help in the selling of the tickets, please get in touch with us, won't you? It will be raffled off on October the 17th, but all money and stubs have to be in by Oct. 10. We sincerely hope all of you will help, so don't let our hopes down.

And in normal fashion, the same letter ends, "That's all for now. Remember V-E day has come and gone, but V-J day is only in sight so keep buying those War Bonds and Stamps."[25]

Mentions of Franklin D. Roosevelt in fan club journals appeared most often in the form of tributes rather than campaign plugs, particularly after his death. The June 1945 issue of *The Sinatra Sender*, published by the Frankies United Swooners club, for example, included the following tribute:

> On April 12th, we lost one of our greatest presidents in history—Franklin Delano Roosevelt. He died to preserve the peace of ours and of the other countries of the world. So that he did not die in vain, let's buy more and more war bonds to guarantee everlasting peace.[26]

While fan club members were not necessarily encouraged to vote for Roosevelt's historic fourth term in the 1944 election, most of them being too young to vote, Sinatra's campaigning for Roosevelt still influenced his young fans. One 1944 article in the *New York Times* suggested that young Sinatra fans listened to Sinatra's political messages with genuine attentiveness and respect, indicating an interest in both current and future political involvement:

---

[23] "We Hear," *Ora e Sempre Sinatra*, Edition 1 (c. Summer 1945), 3, author's collection.
[24] Anne Cassiani, "From the Secretary," *Sinatra-ly Yours* (Fall 1944), 3, Sinatra-ana.
[25] Mildred Schultz and Irene Yourgas, *BowTie Bugle*, no. 7 (Spring 1945): 1, Sinatra-ana.
[26] *The Sinatra Sender* 1, Issue 3 (June 1945): 1.

> Frank Sinatra spoke on President Roosevelt's behalf before a predominantly bobby socks audience in crowded Carnegie Hall last night—spoke gravely, and was heard with marked respect ... there was no hysteria, no swooning, which uneasy adults in the hall clearly expected.[27]

The same article notes that a message from the president was read at this appearance, in which he praised America's youth for their interest in politics and noted the important role they would play in the future direction of the nation.

What is perhaps most notable about Sinatra's political messaging in relation to his fans is the fact that mass media did in fact notice the potential power American teenagers had in influencing the direction of politics, even if they were too young to vote. What's more, some noticed the power of using popular culture figures to further influence this potential. A 1944 issue of *Variety* noticed, "Sinatra is now a hot FDR rooter (he's going on the air Oct. 26 to stump for him) and his kid fans, even though they're not old enough to vote, are following suit. They're all wearing FDR buttons."[28] Another issue of *Variety* covered an event which demonstrated the fact that the US government and film industry together saw potential in using Sinatra as a vehicle for encouraging youth to support the war:

> For the first time since Pearl Harbor, the motion picture industry is mulling plans to glamorize War Bond buyers. According to a campaign under consideration by film industry Sixth War Loan campaign committee heads in New York, one of the earliest appeals in the current drive is to be aimed at bobbysoxers throughout the country via a tieup with Frank Sinatra....
>
> Under the proposal, teen-agers will be given ticket numbers with bond purchases, the winner to be made up "studio style" by Eddie Senz in Times Square, N.Y. Sinatra is to make a personal appearance, launch an appeal to his teenage following to buy more War Bonds, congratulate the winning bobbysoxer, and escort the girl, possibly parents also, as his guest at the Waldorf-Astoria hotel, N.Y.
>
> During the drive for bobbysox bond buyers, girls will be encouraged to bring piggy-banks to Times Square and break them open in view of

---

[27] "Youngsters Flock to Sinatra Speech," *New York Times*, October 25, 1944, 16.
[28] "'Voice' Silenced on FDR Visit Reference as Guest of Benny; Plenty Burned," *Variety*, October 11, 1944, 1.

cameramen covering the event. While the bobbysox brigade has been considered primarily a N.Y. product, bond sellers believe that their equivalent is to be found in homes throughout the country.

The Sinatra stunt, it is pointed out, may be staged in large cities wherever there are expert makeup men to "glamorize" the winners and local matinee idols to serve as escorts.[29]

Although it is not surprising that society assumed teenage girls would only be interested in supporting the war or politics if they were bribed with glamorous experiences and promises of meeting Sinatra, Sinatra fan club journals show that Sinatra's involvement in political and civil issues acted as a catalyst for cultivating genuine interest among teenage girls. E. J. Kahn Jr., writer for the *New Yorker* and author *The Voice: The Story of an American Phenomenon* (one of the earliest published attempts to understand Sinatra's war-era career and fan community), seemed to notice that Sinatra fans appreciated the star not just for his voice and image, but for his supposed substance when it came to expressing his beliefs:

> Sinatra's evolution, in the past two years, into a crusader for civil liberties and a political orator has delighted his fans. They are impressed by the knowledge that they are pledged to an entertainer of such versatility, and they look down upon the more limited idols of other fans. "Van Johnson," one Sinatra fan said in disparagement of an actor who has quite a few fans of his own, "hasn't done a darn thing for anybody except sit around and look cute." While Sinatra was stumping for Roosevelt in 1944, his fans dutifully put on buttons saying, "Frankie's for F.D.R. and so are we," and took to nagging at their parents to vote a straight Sinatra ticket. The Sinatra-fan-club papers run editorials condemning intolerance and urging their readers to cut down on ice-cream sodas so that they can contribute—in Sinatra's name, of course—to humanitarian causes.[30]

Despite widespread public support of Roosevelt, a president championed for his devoted leadership and liberal values, the racial and religious discrimination Americans were battling on the home front continued to be

---

[29] "Sinatra to Sparkplug War Bond Drive to Bobbysoxers; Glamor Pitch," *Variety*, November 8, 1944, 1–31.

[30] E. J. Kahn Jr., *The Voice: The Story of an American Phenomenon* (New York: Harper & Brothers, 1946), 57–58.

exacerbated by wartime fears and quickly shifting mindsets regarding American superiority. Disputes continued as to who exactly was considered to be a true American. As noted, while Sinatra publicly fought discrimination against African Americans, Catholics and Jews, and European immigrants, he did not make equal efforts to defend Japanese Americans, who were swiftly demonized in the American psyche and physically interned after the attack on Pearl Harbor. American nationalism and prejudice was specific in whom and what it targeted. And although American citizens held their own individual ideas regarding these issues, their daily interactions with different "types" of Americans, and especially foreigners, were strongly influenced by the US government. This influence extended to American teenagers, yet the young fans of Frank Sinatra proved to approach these relationships in surprising ways.

Nationalism and the Adopt a Foreign Fan Association

Propaganda was not new in World War II, but the sheer quantity and characteristics of World War II propaganda mark this as a defining period in the distribution of government ideologies through mass media. Of course, when many people think about propaganda in World War II, their minds go straight to that of Nazi Germany, where Adolf Hitler and his minister of propaganda, Joseph Goebbels, headed a massive and intricate system of propaganda messaging to German citizens and the world. The Allied nations, and the United States specifically, however, were far from absent in the culture of wartime propaganda. The US government similarly utilized mass media to spread messages to American citizens on all topics related to war, such as rationing, service, war work, and the dangers that Axis countries posed.

American propaganda campaigns were rooted in the larger context of increased feelings of nationalism within the United States and throughout the world during the war years.[31] In the United States, the government worked to instill in citizens the feeling that American values, strength, and citizens would set the foundation for victory over the Axis powers, who were portrayed as sub-human when compared to Americans and the Allied

---

[31] For more on the nature of American nationalism in the twentieth century, see John Fousek, *To Lead the Free World: American Nationalism & the Cultural Roots of the Cold War* (Chapel Hill: University of North Carolina Press, 2000), 6.

nations. Both the superiority of the American people and the need to restrict interactions with foreigners was at the forefront of many Americans' sense of self and nation during the war years.

While government concerns surrounding civilian roles and responsibilities in maintaining national security were not completely unfounded—it was true that enemy spies could be working to collect information from ignorant American citizens on the home front—the propaganda campaign promoting this issue was intense. Phrases such as "loose lips sink ships," "zip your lip," and "keep mum, chum," were used in media messaging, especially mass-produced posters, to warn citizens that their seemingly innocent gossip with neighbors and colleagues could result in national security breaches. Newspaper coverage of the era reveals the extent to which Americans were subjected to these warnings from the US government, with headlines such as, "A Slip of the Lip Might Sink a Ship,"[32] "Army Office Hits Loose Talk about Military Affairs,"[33] and "'Button Your Lip' Posters Shown at City Hall"[34] running in newspapers throughout the war. One 1943 article in the *Pittsburgh Courier* described US government efforts to curb "loose talk" among American citizens, while still emphasizing that this kind of campaign was different from the kind of propaganda being spread in Nazi Germany:

> Washington, D.C. Jan. 14—The Germans depend entirely on their Gestapo to prevent their people from talking too much, but our system is different. Instead of depending wholly on force, our government is seeking the voluntary co-operation of all the people to see to it that vital information does not get into the hands of the enemy. To this end a campaign is now in progress for the Security of War Information. Through posters, the radio, motion pictures and the press, the idea that loose talk is dangerous is being pushed.[35]

The article continues by providing general rules citizens should follow, including "not to talk about your job in public" and "if you have relatives in the service, don't discuss their whereabouts or movements publicly."[36] Citizens were warned that even casual chat about the weather forecast could provide

---

[32] Alimisha E. Horton, "A Slip of the Lip Might Sink a Ship," *Pittsburgh Courier*, August 15, 1942, 23.
[33] "Army Officer Hits Loose Talk about Military Affairs," *Los Angeles Times*, November 7, 1944, A1.
[34] "'Button Your Lip' Posters Shown at City Hall," *New York Times*, February 18, 1942, 21.
[35] "Loose Talk May Cost Lives, Government Warns," *Pittsburgh Courier*, January 16, 1943, 7.
[36] "Loose Talk May Cost Lives," 7.

enemy spies with crucial information about when would be best to attack, or when the United States might be operating military actions.

Although this national security campaign was directed at all American citizens, posters and other media messages often suggested that the problem of dangerous loose talk was most rampant among women. In a 1942 article in the *Daily Boston Globe*, which described a survey that supposedly revealed Massachusetts citizens as especially bad offenders when it came to talking publicly about the war, the article begins by feminizing the entire state:

> Massachusetts was told yesterday to watch her tongue.
>
> She talks too much!
>
> This was the result of a listening survey of unguarded war talk in public places conducted by the public information division of the Massachusetts Committee on Public Safety....
>
> Gossip at the cocktail lounge, the beauty parlor, the friendly bridge game and conversation over the back fence is mostly concerned with so-called "inside stuff."
>
> Employees of defense plants seem to be the worst offenders, the survey indicates, in talking shop after hours.[37]

Describing Massachusetts as "she" and listing spaces traditionally occupied by women such as beauty parlors and bridge games suggested that women were especially prone to unknowingly revealing war information through gossip. In addition, posters created by this government campaign frequently portrayed stereotypically attractive, innocent-looking women as negligent citizens who could cause the deaths of American troops, working to spread equal parts fear and guilt among those Americans who were supposedly prone to gossip (Figure 3.3 and 3.4).

In this propagandistic context, it is notable that one of America's most overlooked social groups—teenage girls—embraced opportunities to build relationships with their peers in other countries. It is even more notable that they did so in the midst of widespread campaigns to prevent Americans from interacting with strangers, especially foreign strangers. Specifically, the American teenage fans of Frank Sinatra used their love of the pop idol to connect with other young Sinatra fans all over the world, building international

---

[37] "Bay Staters Too Talkative, Survey Shows: Defense Workers Worst Offenders in OCD Checkup," *Daily Boston Globe*, April 1, 1942, 13.

Figure 3.3 Victor Keppler, artist. Adjutant General's Office (1944). New Hampshire State Library.

pen-pal relationships with foreign fans on a large scale. Significantly, these relationships were encouraged and facilitated by one of Sinatra's own employees, suggesting Sinatra himself supported this kind of international communication.

It is not surprising that most Frank Sinatra fan club members, or any Sinatra fan in general, would never meet Sinatra in person, or necessarily even see him perform live. As with most celebrities, Sinatra's actual interactions with his fans were mostly limited to avoiding being smothered by them after performances. Most celebrities, including Sinatra, did not—and still do not—respond directly to fan mail, engage directly with fan clubs dedicated to them, or meet with fans in person, except perhaps as part of a publicity engagement.

Despite the lack of contact fans generally had with Sinatra himself, members of Sinatra fan clubs were still able to feel connected with Sinatra's inner world, largely through his personal secretary and fan club liaison, Marjorie Diven.

Figure 3.4 Harry Anderson, artist. US Government Printing Office (1943). New Hampshire State Library.

As a member of Sinatra's staff (who interestingly worked previously in a similar role for Rudy Vallée), Diven's name did not appear very much in public, and outside of Sinatra's fan communities, her contributions to the Sinatra fan experience remain largely unknown. Diven's impact on Sinatra's fans, and especially within his fan clubs, however, was crucial in the development of the imagined relationships fans built with Sinatra and each other.

One of the few places Diven's name appeared in a large-scale publication was in E. J. Kahn Jr.'s 1946 examination of Sinatra's career. Of Diven, Kahn writes:

> [Sinatra] maintains liaison with most of the Sinatra fans through an energetic woman named Marjorie Diven, who sits in a cluttered cubicle stacked to the ceiling with scrapbooks, photographs, card files, and unanswered fan mail. Many Sinatra fans would consider it a treat to be permitted to

help Mrs. Diven paste up clippings and slit envelopes, but ordinarily only fan club presidents enjoy the privilege.... Sinatra's fans have huge respect for Mrs. Diven, and she has been elected to honorary membership in hundreds of their clubs.... Marj, who some years ago acted as a buffer between Rudy Vallée and his admirers, has been handling Frank's fans for George [Evans] since the spring of 1944. Hers is so much a labor of love that she keeps at it nights and weekends.

"People think it's strange that I take this business so seriously," she says, "but I've seen many things it does that go beyond the eye."[38]

While much of the content in Kahn's book is hard to confirm as fact or speculation, there is no question that Marjorie Diven did treat her role very seriously and was committed to ensuring that Sinatra's fans felt connected and involved with Sinatra's career, because she knew fans were key to his success. Fan clubs in turn often felt they were not "official" until they had received correspondence from Diven and had been added to her list of active clubs. One letter to club members from Frank Sinatra Music Club president, Frances Bergstrom, indicated that their club was ready to move forward after contacting Diven. Bergstrom wrote, "The FS Music Club is out of Miss Diven's inactive file now that this journal is distributed, and we are ready to go ahead with club plans for the summer."[39] Frequent mentions of "Miss Diven," "Marjorie Diven," "Marj," and "Sinatra's secretary" are made throughout Sinatra fan club publications and individual correspondence, highlighting how valued Diven was in Sinatra's fan communities.

One of the most notable initiatives Diven created for Sinatra's fan club communities involved not only Sinatra's American fans, but his fans from all over the world. Of course, many American celebrities had international fans and vice versa, but what was distinct about Marjorie Diven was the way she strove to make Sinatra's foreign fans feel that they were just as important to Sinatra himself as his fans in the United States were. This was especially notable in the context of international warfare and extreme censorship and propaganda programs warning American citizens not to speak with foreigners.

Diven's primary achievement in creating connections between Sinatra's American and foreign fans was the development of the Adopt a Foreign Fan

---

[38] Kahn, *The Voice*, 69–71.
[39] Frances Bergstrom, "Notes to Frank Sinatra Music Club Members," c. 1945, Sinatra-ana.

Association (AAFFA). Diven created the AAFFA with the intention both to encourage friendly relationships between international fans and to field the overwhelming amount of interest and letters she was receiving from foreign fans. Unsurprisingly, fans from Axis nations were not included in this initiative. The nations that were included, however, proved to reach much further than just the United States' closest allies (although letters from England made up a large portion of AAFFA correspondence). Semper Sinatra Club president Irene Di Mattia, for example, indicated in a letter to gossip columnist, Hedda Hopper, that their club members were in contact with and included fans from multiple countries, not just England:

> A little while back you mentioned that there were Sinatra fans in England but they didn't get much of a chance to see his movies. However, I have had letters from English fans who have seen *Anchors Aweigh* as much as 25 times. I thought you might be interested in the fact that our fan club has members in Hawaii, Canada, England, Ireland, Palestine, Sweden and South Africa.[40]

While Di Mattia's letter was written after the war's end, the success of the AAFFA during the war can be seen in Sinatra fan club journals, where club members published letters and information from Diven alongside their own ideas and responses to her work. The first edition of *Ora e Sempre Sinatra*, published by the Ora e Sempre Sinatra club, included a letter from Diven explaining the purpose of the AAFFA and encouraging club members to participate:

> Following is a part of a letter I received from Marjorie Diven, Frank's secretary. This part explains what I think to be a very good plan. Read it thoroughly and I'm sure you'll agree.
> "This plan, which I put into action a couple of months ago, is a way to bring the foreign fans and the American fans together. . . . They all want to know about Frank and nobody was telling them anything. I couldn't begin to write to half of them, and Frank doesn't even have a chance to write to the fans here.

---

[40] Irene Di Mattia to Hedda Hopper, April 2, 1947, Hedda Hopper papers, Margaret Herrick Library, Academy of Motion Picture Arts and Sciences, Beverly Hills, CA. Originally quoted in Katie Beisel Hollenbach, "Teenage Agency and Popular Music Reception in World War II–Era Frank Sinatra Fan Clubs," *Journal of Popular Music Studies* 31, no. 4 (2019): 159.

"So I formed the 'Adopt a Foreign Fan Association,' which is composed of fan club presidents in this country. To each club president (AAFFA member) I send a list of foreign fans, as many names as she has members in the club. She gives one name to each member, for the member to write to. She 'adopts' the fan in her care, she asks her to be a pen-pal and offering to tell her all about Frank. Some of them send extra snaps or whatever they can spare.

"In a way, it is better than having the foreign fans join our club as the question of dues is very awkward. This way costs practically nothing to anyone. I send out a monthly bulletin to members and as soon as the foreign AAFFA group is developed sufficiently, they will get a special bulletin just for them."

She then goes on to explain how she got in touch with these people. She already has established set-ups in Ireland, England, Africa, and British Guiana.

If you are interested in this plan drop me a card saying where you would like a pen-pal....

Let's show our interest and be among the other Frank Sinatra Fan Clubs who are spreading news of our favorite.

Nonie[41]

Another feature in the Summer 1945 edition of *Sinatra-ly Yours*, published by the Semper Sinatra club, contains a similar letter from Diven that emphasizes her desire to make sure Sinatra's foreign fans do not feel like they are a lower priority than his American fans:

Frank gets loads of foreign mail, not only from service men but from regular fans. It is the fans I'm talking about now. I checked my files and find that Frank has received fan mail from 33 countries. They are mostly from England and the next biggest is Australia, where they are wild about Frank. Frank never gets a chance to write letters and my hands are full with an enormous U.S. correspondence, yet these overseas admirers are left out in the cold—they can't see him at broadcasts and shows and they don't get the information they want. So I formed the AAFFA which means the "Adopt a Foreign Fan Association" and is composed of club presidents in this country. There are now 21 members.

---

[41] Nonie (last name unknown), *Ora e Sempre Sinatra*, Edition 1 (c. 1945), 4, author's collection.

To each club president I give as many foreign names as there are members in the club and she gives just ONE name to each member. This foreign fan is then "adopted" by the girl who draws her name. The member writes, asking her to be a penpal and offering to tell her all about Frank. Some of them are offering to send snaps. This gets around the idea of making them regular members as the club can't afford to send the paper and the matter of dues is too awkward. Some put the announcement in the club paper and they work out various schemes to distribute the names to the members.

The club members are delighted with the idea. One club is taking Scotland only—200 members in that club. Others want their pals in mixed countries, but I'd mostly like to see the English girls get penpals.[42]

The matter of what fan club members should write about in their letters to foreign fans was also discussed both in letters from Marjorie Diven and among club members themselves. Conspicuously absent is any talk of the war itself. Rather, club members were encouraged to write about their own interests and of course Sinatra, and to ask the same of their foreign pen pals. This certainly could have stemmed from US propaganda initiatives that warned citizens of sharing information that could dangerously affect the war effort, but Sinatra fans seemed genuinely more interested in learning about the lives of their pen pals outside of the war. It is not hard to imagine that, within the war-consumed daily lives all of these fans were living, they preferred to briefly set aside talk of the war in favor of building international relationships based on mutual interests and their love of Sinatra instead. One letter from Diven to the Sing with the Sinatras club demonstrates this mindset:

What should go into the first letter? The purpose of the letter is to make a new friend. Tell her about yourself and where you live and ask her about herself. Find out whether she has seen Frank's movies, heard the broadcasts or what. Tell her about such things as the Paramount [and] the Waldorf if you've visited these places. If not draw on your scrapbooks for information or quote from other club papers. The overseas fans do not always express themselves so ardently as we do, so 'till you know her better avoid too much slang. She will wonder how you got her name, so tell her of the AAFFA and

---

[42] Marjorie Diven, quoted in "Excerpts from Letter Received from Frank's Secretary," *Sinatra-ly Yours* (Summer 1945), 3, Sinatra-ana.

that Frank really does like to get letters even tho the pressure of so much keeps him from writing.

When replies are received? Who should we tell? Report anything of interest to your own fan club prexy. And don't forget me! I want to know all about everything. There's fun in store for all of you, so let's go!

Sinatra-lly yours

Marjorie Diven, secretary to F. Sinatra.[43]

Fan club members proved to show great enthusiasm for the AAFFA, with many including reminders to members in club journals to get involved and share their experiences with their fellow members. The Sing with the Sinatras club was especially adamant in their participation in the AAFFA, and the club's president, Juanita Stephens, often asked members to share as much about their foreign pen pals as possible. Stephens shared her own positive experience in the December 1945 issue of the *T-Jacket Journal* in the hopes of encouraging more members to participate:

It was raining and I'd just barely passed an Algebra ex. So my spirits were pretty low when I came in that day. Waiting for me was a letter from Rita Jenkinson, fresh from Eng. and some movie mags from another FF [foreign fan] Syliva Sears [sic], immediately my spirits sored [sic]. Why I was feeling so good the next day, that I made 'A' on a Shakespeare test. Next month if possible I'd like to ask Mary Lee Sullivan to write a paragraph or two about her Foreign fan and how she likes the AAFFA. Some fun, hey![44]

Members of the Sing with the Sinatras club must have continued to increase their participation in the AAFFA, as Stephens regularly published updates about the organization in other issues of the *T-Jacket Journal* and eventually created an organized system for members to report their experiences:

All of you received the address of a foreign fan when you joined. Now I hope they can be called not only Frank's foreign fans, but your friends. Will all of you please make a report (on a separate piece of paper) including the answers to the following:

---

[43] Marjorie Diven, quoted in "AAFFA Bulletin No. 1," *T-Jacket Journal*, Issue 5 (February–March 1946), 3, Rose MARBL.

[44] Juanita Stephens, *T-Jacket Journal* (December 1945), 2, Rose MARBL.

1. Your Name—Your F. Fans name.
2. Did he or she answer your first letter promptly?
3. Approximately how many letters have you written? Received?
4. Would you care for another pen pal?
5. Anything about them or what they have written that would be of interest.

THIS IS IMPORTANT[45]

The journal also began to include features on individual foreign pen pals so other club members could learn more about them. One example featured a pen pal from London, England:

> EILEEN NAYLOR: LONDON, ENGLAND. Swell. That's the only word that can describe my pen pal, Eileen Naylor. I have been writing to her for six months now and she is really grand.... If you don't have a pen pal you'd better get one soon before you miss any more fun.
>
> Helen Frances Reid[46]

This celebration of international fan relationships along with the ideas Sinatra's fans expressed regarding equity and politics in the United States suddenly make media portrayals of teenage girls, such as *Swooner Crooner*, seem out of touch. While mass media coverage of Sinatra usually chose to focus on those fans who participated in mob hysteria at his live performances—and it is true that these mob occurrences did happen sometimes—the reality of most Sinatra fans was one of more nuanced fandom. Yes, these girls adored Sinatra, but the communities they created around this adoration were equally valuable to them as spaces where they could develop their personal ideas and values as American citizens living during World War II. In many ways, these fan communities helped to shape the identities of American teenage girls as they prepared to enter postwar adulthood.

Similarly, wartime media representations of Frank Sinatra as nothing more than a scrawny, sentimental idol of American girls only scraped the surface of Sinatra's celebrity identity and influence. Examining Sinatra's experiences growing up as an Italian American sheds light on the set of

---

[45] "AAFFA News," *T-Jacket Journal* (June–July 1946), 3, Rose MARBL.
[46] Helen Frances Reid, "Let's Meet Some Foreign Fans," *T-Jacket Journal* (April–May 1946), 3, Rose MARBL.

political and social values he developed and publicly expressed during the war years, which in turn strongly influenced those values of his young fans. Some media coverage did acknowledge Sinatra's public efforts in preaching tolerance and liberal politics, but as with his teenage fans, most chose instead to emphasize a more superficial version of the star.

Conclusion

While Sinatra's young fans proved to use their fandom as a platform for engaging in public issues, this does not mean they neglected the core thing that initially brought them together—adoration of Sinatra. As this chapter has explored the ways Sinatra's admirers brought their fandom into the public sphere, the next chapter will look inward at the ways fans expressed more personal desires and opinions regarding Sinatra and music in general, within their fan club communities. In an era when women were discouraged from publicly displaying their sexuality and desires—and female sexuality was even regulated by the government in some instances—Sinatra fan clubs provided a space where teenage girls could share and explore these feelings with understanding peers, away from the public eye.

4
Fans as Critics and Material Culture Makers

In the introduction to *The Cambridge History of Music Criticism*, Christopher Dingle makes the following important yet often forgotten observation: "All histories are partial. All histories are simplifications. . . . Even before considering the prejudices, philosophy or political intent of the author, history is written from a particular perspective, at a particular time, with access to particular evidence."[1] This may seem relatively obvious at first glance, but Dingle was prudent to preface a collection of essays on the history of music criticism with this reminder, as we see clear evidence of the marginalization of certain people, genres, and perspectives in this history.

What and whom do most people picture when they think of music criticism? Perhaps they think of reviews of prestigious concerts published in the "Arts" section of the *New York Times* by established writers. Those who are familiar with Western music history may think of the famous European music critics from the eighteenth and nineteenth centuries who combined music criticism with philosophy. Or maybe popular music reviews found in the glossy pages of *Rolling Stone* magazine come to mind. The practice of music criticism is one that spans multiple centuries and has adapted to such cultural developments as world wars, mass media, and digitization, yet there remain certain constants in this history. Namely, that it is an overwhelmingly male history and one that strongly values texts written by professional critics in commercial and academic publications over texts written by non-professionals in more private spaces. Even in genres such as rock criticism, which, when compared to other forms of music criticism, has been viewed as anti-academic, subjective, and sometimes shocking (e.g., as in the case of rock critic Lester Bangs), the history is still male-dominated and public-facing.[2]

---

[1] Christopher Dingle, "Introduction," in *The Cambridge History of Music Criticism* (Cambridge: Cambridge University Press, 2019), 1.

[2] For an overview of rock criticism see Ulf Lindberg, Gestur Guðmundsson, Morten Michelsen, and Hans Weisethaunet, *Rock Criticism from the Beginning: Amusers, Bruisers, & Cool-Headed Cruisers* (New York: Peter Lang, 2005).

Although there are notable exceptions of prominent women musicians and composers in the history of Western music, the history of music criticism still displays a significant lack in the representation of women, and especially those women who pursued musical practices outside of the public sphere.

The lack of women's representation in music history and criticism in turn affects how scholars can study certain historical moments using methodologies of reception. Because women's voices are often difficult to locate in historical publications and other artifacts, it can be challenging to recreate what Hans Robert Jauss coined a "horizon of expectations" from female perspectives. In reception theories, the "horizon of expectations" describes the system of references, expectations, and experiences an individual possesses that affects how they interpret cultural texts, including art, literature, and music.[3] In Jauss's words, reconstructing these systems allows scholars to "pose questions that the text gave an answer to, and thereby to discover how the contemporary reader could have viewed and understood the work."[4] Historical music criticism has increasingly been seen as a rich and obvious source by musicologists for approaching music through the lens of reception, as Dingle mentions, but again, these sources have largely come from male perspectives, posing limitations on our understandings of music history.[5]

While some histories of women musicians and composers exist, and more continue to be written, locating histories of women audiences or women who practiced music in the private rather than public sphere is especially difficult. As Marcia J. Citron's landmark work on gender and reception describes, this is largely because "female interpretive communities have typically operated outside the mainstream and beyond the reach of the professional critic."[6] In other words, not only have private women's musical practices been overlooked in favor of male-dominated public musical cultures, but access to the materials these kinds of communities produced is limited, making it even more challenging to bring these histories to light. The issue of access to material culture is one reason fan criticism in particular has only just recently begun to find its way into scholarship, yet

---

[3] Robert C. Holub, *Reception Theory: A Critical Introduction* (London: Methuen, 1984), 59.
[4] Hans Robert Jauss, *Toward an Aesthetic of Reception*, trans. Timothy Bahti (Minneapolis: University of Minnesota Press, 1982), 28.
[5] Dingle, "Introduction," 1.
[6] Marcia J. Citron, *Gender and the Musical Canon* (Cambridge: Cambridge University Press, 1993), 188.

the potential to discover new historical narratives from fan-made texts is significant.[7]

Scholarship on fanzines, for example, has continued to find a more prominent place in fan studies, though most focuses on zines from around the 1970s on, usually crediting science fiction fan communities as the point of zine origin. Work on zines in music is perhaps most prominent in studies of punk and Riot Grrrl movements, in which self-publication was arguably as important to the movements' missions as music was.[8] Kevin Dunn and May Summer Farnsworth, for example, describe how zines reflected the anti-establishment sentiment at play in punk and Riot Grrrl circles, noting, "The DIY ethos reflects an intentional transformation of punks from consumers of the mass media to agents of cultural production."[9]

As with most music criticism, attention to publications made by fan communities skew toward those with primarily male membership, Riot Grrrl zines being a notable exception. As scholars such as Norma Coates have noted, this trend stems in part from a historical assumption that female, and especially young female, cultural perspectives hold less value and sophistication than those of males. Coates describes this mindset in reference to 1960s and 1970s teenyboppers: "What unites [teenyboppers] is their bad taste, as perceived by the critics and scholars who 'know better.' ... One other thing characterizes the discursive teenybopper, her femaleness."[10] Considering texts created by female fans, however, is important for understanding how girl cultures operate within larger societal frameworks of gender and youth politics.[11]

In terms of understanding the lives of American teenage girls during World War II, consulting the texts they made through their popular culture fandom reveals these modes of self-expression and demonstrates how teenage girls

---

[7] Recent examples of scholarship that includes fan criticism include Candy Leonard, *Beatleness: How the Beatles and Their Fans Remade the World* (New York: Arcade Publishing, 2014); and Allison McCracken, *Real Men Don't Sing: Crooning in American Culture* (Durham, NC: Duke University Press, 2015).

[8] Examples include Paula Guerra and Pedro Quintela, eds., *Punk, Fanzines and DIY Cultures in a Global World: Fast, Furious and Xerox* (Cham: Palgrave Macmillan, 2020); and The Subcultures Network, *Ripped, Torn and Cut: Pop, Politics and Punk Fanzines from 1976* (Manchester: Manchester University Press, 2018).

[9] Kevin Dunn and May Summer Farnsworth, "'We ARE the Revolution': Riot Grrrl Press, Girl Empowerment, and DIY Self-Publishing," *Women's Studies* 41, no. 2 (2012): 144.

[10] Norma Coates, "Teenyboppers, Groupies, and Other Grotesques: Girls and Women in Rock Culture in the 1960s and early 1970s," *Journal of Popular Music Studies* 15, no. 1 (2003): 68.

[11] For more on Riot Grrrl and girl youth cultures, see Joanne Gottlieb and Gayle Wald, "Smells Like Teen Spirit: Riot Grrrls, Revolution and Women in Independent Rock," in *Microphone Fiends: Youth Music & Youth Culture*, ed. Andrew Ross and Tricia Rose (New York: Routledge, 1994).

acted as music critics, not only through traditional reviews and commentary of musicians and recordings, but also through original creative works such as essays and poetry. Studying these fan-made objects provides new clarity into how teenage girls used popular music to navigate their overwhelming World War II lives and sheds light on this monumental period in American women's history.

Through examination of fan-written texts and creative objects both in commercial fan magazines of the 1940s and independent fan club journals, particularly those dedicated to Frank Sinatra, we can gain a new understanding of the values, concerns, and desires teenage girls experienced and expressed through their fandom. In addition, this chapter will consider the participation of those few male members of Frank Sinatra fan clubs, which suggest these clubs also provided space for males who were experiencing feelings of vulnerability to express that in an era when American men and boys were taught to exhibit emotional strength. Of course, these accounts from this fan community represent a "particular perspective, at a particular time, with access to particular evidence," as Dingle reminds us, but it is optimistically one that introduces new voices into the history of World War II popular culture.

"Speak for Yourself": Reader Participation in Commercial Fan Magazines

As noted in Chapter 2, scholarship on fan-made texts before the advent of the internet has often focused on fanzines, fan fiction, and other creations that have largely operated "underground," away from the public eye. And while teenage music and film fans in the 1940s created materials that were intended to be seen only by their specific fan communities, they also contributed their ideas for publication in large-scale commercial magazines. This is one notable way in which this fan community differs from others found in scholarship, such as the Riot Grrrl movement, which maintained an anti-establishment, anti-mass media position.[12] The fan communities of war-era stars, and Frank Sinatra specifically, operated both in and out of the public sphere, interacting privately with each other through fan club

---

[12] See Gottlieb and Wald, "Smells Like Teen Spirit," for more on the relationship between the Riot Grrrl movement and commercial media such as *Sassy* magazine.

journals and publicly with commercial organizations such as the Modern Screen Fan Club Association. This dual discourse encourages the opportunity to examine how fandom served wartime teenage girls not only in their private lives, but as active participants in the shaping of popular culture at large.

Space for readers to contribute their ideas about popular culture was found most often in movie fan magazines. While these magazines were primarily dedicated to films and screen celebrities, popular music was often the subject of articles and reader reviews, in large part because many of the decade's biggest film stars were also the biggest music stars. The enormous popularity of film musicals meant that many popular figures performed double duty as singers and actors. Artists such as Bing Crosby, Judy Garland, Gene Kelly, Frank Sinatra, and Kathryn Grayson fell into this category and cultivated fan bases that admired them both on film and radio and records.

Once again, it is important to note the matter of representation in the content of these fan magazines and the stars they featured. As noted in the Introduction, representation in most commercial fan magazines such as *Modern Screen*, *Photoplay*, and *Screenland* was limited to coverage of white stars, with advertisements that portrayed white American female consumers. This is not to say that these magazines were never consumed by readers of underrepresented races and ethnicities (exact readership was difficult to track, as after initial purchase, magazines could be picked up and circulated from most any public space, such as the street, beauty parlors, public transportation, etc.). This alienation of non-white readers does suggest, however, that most readers of these magazines were likely white.[13]

In terms of reader write-ins to these magazines, however, the question of anonymity is also again relevant to consider, as despite some assumptions that most reader write-ins to magazines were fabricated by magazine editors, many write-ins were in fact genuine. This is shown in part by mentions in fan club journals of members seeing their own contributions or those of their friends appear in magazines. Reader write-ins were of course likely edited before publication, but in reference to radio fan magazines specifically, Elena Razlogova makes an important point, noting, "Radio fan magazines printed readers' opinions in columns entitled 'Voice of the Listener' and 'The

---

[13] More information on African American women's representation in mass media can be found in Maureen Honey, *Bitter Fruit: African American Women in World War II* (Columbia: University of Missouri Press, 1999).

Listener Speaks." Marketing drove much of this, but ideas did circulate, letters were written, sent, read, and answered. Broadcasters did not conjure up their listening public with a throw of a switch. The public participated in its own making."[14] The same can be said of movie fan magazines of the era.

In dialogue with the question of anonymity in Frank Sinatra fan clubs found in Chapter 2, we can consider the possibility that by not publishing readers' photographs or other personal information aside from name, location, and sometimes age in write-in sections, these magazines could have created space for underrepresented minorities to comfortably submit their opinions. Again though, the level at which non-white readers would have participated is difficult to gauge, since these readers were not well represented in other areas of these magazines.

Despite these limits in representation and challenges in pinpointing exact readership, reader write-in sections nevertheless reveal insight into what American women and girls—the main targeted audience of these magazines—prioritized and valued in popular culture media.

We have already seen in Chapter 2 how the entertainment industry, and fan magazines especially, encouraged fans to interact directly with commercial organizations to create a feeling of partnership in the shaping of American popular culture, whether or not this kind of power really was shared with fans. The important thing for fan magazines was that fans *felt* their opinions were being valued by entertainment professionals, as this feeling led to a stronger desire to continue purchasing magazines and the products they advertised. Fans, and especially members of celebrity fan clubs, in turn felt a sense of duty to support their favorite stars by sharing their opinions directly with magazines and radio and studio executives.[15]

Examples of audience opinions in fan magazines are most easily found in those that included regular features dedicated to reader letters. *Photoplay* magazine (1911–1980), for example, included a regular column titled "Speak for Yourself," in which readers were encouraged to send their opinions in exchange for cash prizes. Submissions ranged from enthusiastic praise to harsh criticisms and lists of demands. Musical stars and films were frequently mentioned, such as in a glowing letter in the November 1944 issue from

---

[14] Elena Razlogova, *The Listener's Voice: Early Radio and the American Public* (Philadelphia: University of Pennsylvania Press, 2011), 9.

[15] Samantha Barbas, *Movie Crazy: Fans, Stars, and the Cult of Celebrity* (New York: Palgrave, 2001), 134.

L. Smith of Pittsburgh, Pennsylvania, who wrote of Bing Crosby, "He has a way of singing that touches the hearts of his vast audiences."[16] In a less positive letter in the June 1943 issue, Loretta McCabe of Newark, New Jersey wrote, "If I had my way . . . Betty Grable's option would be dropped; a hummingbird sings better than she does, anyway."[17]

Similarly, *Screenland* magazine (1920–1971) featured a column titled "Fan's Forum." In the July 1943 issue, Betty Aldrich of Austin, Texas, provided the following advice for producers of film musicals: "Ration the big name bands for those tremendous musicals, so as to feature only one or two at a time, instead of the dozen or so usually jammed into one picture."[18] One letter in the May 1943 issue (Figure 4.1) from Marilyn Franz of Manitowoc, Wisconsin, praised a performance by Kathryn Grayson while making a request to producers:

> I should like to submit my letter in your monthly contest. (I'm only fifteen.)
>
> After a week of cramming and semester exams, the gang decided that what we needed was a little fun. . . . We were so completely enchanted by pert Kathryn Grayson and handsome Van Heflin that we didn't even think of the outcome of the history exam. Instead, we hummed the catchy melodies from the film and praised the super performances of the *Seven Sweethearts* and their friends.
>
> It was such a friendly picture, so charming and gay, that we all felt the need of thanking someone for it. Perhaps this is the best way. However, we would also like to ask that Hollywood give us many more pictures like *Seven Sweethearts*.[19]

All of these letters indicate that fans believed their opinions were valued enough by entertainment executives that it was worth their time to write them. And while the criticism offered in these letters was not always very specific and looked markedly different from criticism published by professional music and film critics, they can be used as a source of insight into the values of wartime young women and girls. From just this small sampling of fan letters, we can see that audiences valued such entertainment

[16] L. Smith. "Cheer for Crosby," *Photoplay* (November 1944), 4.
[17] Loretta McCabe, "It Could Happen," *Photoplay* (June 1943), 14.
[18] Betty Aldrich, letter in "Fan's Forum," *Screenland* (July 1943), 14.
[19] Marilyn Franz, letter in "Fan's Forum," *Screenland* (May 1943), 14.

Figure 4.1 "Fan's Forum" in *Screenland*. May 1943. Media History Digital Library.

elements as high-quality musical performances, quality over quantity in musicals, and celebrity performances that felt sincere and connected with audiences.

The letters published in fan magazines provide insight into the entertainment values of female audience members, but texts produced entirely by fans themselves, particularly fan club journals, provide much more detailed and less mediated examples of fan criticism in different forms, including essays, reviews, and poetry.

Creative Criticism in Fan-Made Texts

> There is something about Frank Sinatra that is so pleasingly informal and yet so very different. I like his way of making each girl think he is singing directly to her. There is something in his voice that sounds sincere, as if he really means what he sings. Not only his singing voice, but his talking voice too seems warm and full of meaning.[20]

In the June 1946 issue of *Sinatra Scope*, published by the Frank Sinatra Music Club, member Beth Hurwitz contributed a short essay titled "Why I Like Frank Sinatra." The essay began with the above description of what Hurwitz enjoyed about Sinatra's voice and continued with other characteristics she admired such as his appearance and activism. Hurwitz, who was twelve years old in August 1945, was one of the youngest members of the club, yet she contributed frequently to the club journal.

The commentary Hurwitz provides regarding Sinatra's voice may not initially strike contemporary readers as music criticism. She does not include specialized musical terms in her review that a professional music critic may use, nor does she mention a specific performance or recording. In addition, it feels safe to assume that most people, both in the 1940s and today, would not picture a twelve- or thirteen-year-old girl when imagining what the typical music critic looks like. But what exactly defines a music critic, or music criticism? This is a question that has received increasing attention in scholarship, opening new doors to analyzing how, when, and by whom the history of music is recorded and received.

Christopher Dingle writes of critics, "their *raison d'être* is to have opinions, to raise their heads above the parapet and state what they think, within a very limited number of words."[21] If this is the case, we can most definitely view fans, and for that matter anyone who finds value in having, documenting, and sharing opinions, as critics, despite their absence from professional music criticism platforms. In addition, while the challenge of balancing subjective analysis with objective, "poetic" interpretation has been described

---

[20] Beth Hurwitz, "Why I Like Frank Sinatra," *Sinatra Scope* 1, no. 1 (June 1946): 10, Sinatra-ana Collection, Hoboken Historical Museum, Hoboken, NJ (hereafter cited as Sinatra-ana). Used with permission of the author.

[21] Dingle, "Introduction," 2.

as a "major problem" in the history of music criticism,[22] Sinatra fans instead emphasized and found value in both their analytical and emotional responses to Sinatra, in turn revealing more of Sinatra's cultural impact.

Frank Sinatra fan club journals and club member correspondence from the 1940s are packed not only with information regarding club roles and management, as was demonstrated in Chapter 2, but also with fan criticism and opinions regarding popular music, film, and culture in general. Notably, fans expressed their opinions in various formats. Traditional music and film reviews were submitted, but club members also transcribed their thoughts using essays, narrative re-enactments of Sinatra's performances, original poetry, and personal letters to one another. These texts reveal that in addition to appreciating specific musical qualities, fans valued artists who fostered personal connections and expressions of vulnerability.

Because what we might call traditional reviews of music and film appeared frequently in Sinatra fan club journals, we can assume that similar to the fan letters in commercial fan magazines described above, fans valued and sought out high-quality performances and musicianship. Although most of the reviews found in Sinatra fan club journals, especially those of Sinatra himself, were usually positive, members did not refrain from sharing when they felt a performance was not up to standard. For example, in the fifth issue of the Sing with the Sinatras Club journal, the *T-Jacket Journal*, an unnamed member wrote of the 1945 musical film *Doll Face*, "Plot was poor, music was pretty good and the actors did try. [Perry] Como doesn't look as good as he sounds."[23] Like this review, most Sinatra fan club journals included information and reviews about music and films in general, not just those featuring Sinatra. The September 1944 issue of *The Voice*, published by the Slaves of Sinatra club, featured a column titled "The Bandstand," in which member Ginnie (last name not indicated) described the latest musical films members should look out for:

> Hi! again kids [*sic*]. There is another column on the doings of the entertainment world.
> Hope you like it. Any suggestions will be welcome. Write in care of your prexy . . . here we go. . . . The new pictures that have some swell music in them are sure to please all of you. They look pretty good from where I sit.

---

[22] Lindberg, Guðmundsson, Michelsen, and Weisethaunet, *Rock Criticism from the Beginning*, 15.
[23] "Movie Raters," *T-Jacket Journal* (February–March 1946), 10, Stuart A. Rose Manuscript, Archives, and Rare Book Library, Emory University, Atlanta, GA (hereafter cited as Rose MARBL).

Irish Eyes Are Smiling has that pretty wonderful fellow Dick Haymes, who sings his way thru just to let you know Frank Sinatra isn't the only crooner in the world. He does a swell job and his girl is June Haver. Dick plays the part of the composer, Ernest Ball, whose songs all America has sung at one time. I'm sure you'll like it.[24]

She continues with similar descriptions of films such as *Sweet and Low-Down* (Twentieth Century–Fox, 1944) and *Meet Me in St. Louis* (MGM, 1944).

In the April–May 1946 issue of the *T-Jacket Journal*, member Jean Palmer reviewed and recommended popular records to fellow members in the journal's regular column, "Platter Praddle." Palmer writes such comments as "'Gee, It's Good to Hold You' by Woody Herman features a torchy vocal with a good alto-sax" and "For albums we have 'After Dark,' [*sic*] these are some of the old favorites such as 'Stardust,' 'Dancing in the Dark,' 'Temptation,' and many more, the orchestration is by Morton Gould."[25] While these reviews may not reflect the length or descriptive detail that a published review from a professional music critic would generally show, they still demonstrate that teenage club members of Sinatra fan clubs were aware and receptive of such musical elements as vocal quality, musicianship, and orchestration.

Club members also reviewed music and performances in personal correspondence with each other, often with more detail and frankness than in reviews they submitted for their club journals. One notable example can be found in a letter from Esther Bergquist of Minneapolis, Minnesota, to Beth Hurwitz, whose essay "Why I Like Frank Sinatra" was mentioned above. In this letter, Bergquist writes a full page of her opinions regarding Al Jolson and Frank Sinatra, which seem to be in response to a letter from Hurwitz that likely mentioned the 1946 biopic of Al Jolson, *The Jolson Story*. Bergquist's opinions are worth quoting in length:

To me, there is something about Jolson that is sort of "corny" and almost "fishy," and how I dislike using that word! Here is a star—Jolson—who is able to cash in on talent that doesn't sound any better on records now then [*sic*] when he was in his "prime" in showbusiness in the old days. Believe me, I'm not criticizing his age! He never had what Larry Parks has in

---

[24] Ginnie (last name unknown), "The Bandstand," *The Voice* 1, no. 3 (September 1944): 4, Sinatra-ana.
[25] Jean Palmer, "Platter Praddle," *T-Jacket Journal* (April–May 1946), 5, Rose MARBL.

charm, or anything like that. I'll bet that if I think any better of Jolson's style when I see the movie [*The Jolson Story*] it will be because of Larry Parks.

I think it all depends on how you like to hear a song sung, and you wouldn't be being disloyal to Sinatra or any singer for that matter for suddenly deciding you liked the way someone else sings, better (aren't there a lot of S's in that sentence!).

I'm not saying Sinatra is the best ballad singer anymore than he is my favorite singer. But it's my opinion that his balladering [sic] is less tiresome to listen to then [sic] the way some crooners sing a ballad straight and without enough feeling.

Jolson sings carefree—maybe—and that helps to give an impression that the song is the most important thing to him at the moment. That does not necessarily mean he sings a song the way it should be sung, though.[26]

Bergquist's letter reveals that while skill in vocal technique and quality was important to her when listening to popular singers, what she seemed to value most in the music and singers she listened to were performances that felt expressive and genuine. Her description of Jolson, which can be described as subjective and emotional (and a little harsh) yet supported by a sense of genuine interest in musicality, almost seems to foreshadow popular and rock music criticism trends that would be seen decades later.[27]

Sinatra was often credited throughout his career as being particularly talented in achieving the kind of authenticity in his performances that Bergquist describes. As Roger Gilbert notes, "Listening to Sinatra at his best, it's impossible not to feel one is being admitted to the singer's innermost psyche."[28] Criticism and descriptions of performances found in Sinatra fan club journals demonstrate that this was a common value among most club members, not only because it helped foster a feeling of connection with Sinatra, but also because by sharing these values with fellow fans, teenage girls could connect with one another.

While Sinatra's expressions of vulnerability and authenticity in his wartime performances were defining factors in his popularity among teenage

---

[26] Esther Bergquist to Beth Hurwitz (February 8, 1947), Hoboken Historical Museum.

[27] The rock critic Lester Bangs, for example, commercially published criticism that was known for being severely honest and peppered with colorful language and personal opinions, yet rooted in a deep understanding of and passion for music. For examples, see *Mainlines, Blood Feasts, and Bad Taste: A Lester Bangs Reader*, ed. John Morthland (New York: Anchor, 2003).

[28] Roger Gilbert, "Beloved and Notorious: A Theory of American Stardom, with Special Reference to Bing Crosby and Frank Sinatra," *Southwest Review* 95, no. 1/2 (2010): 180.

girls, this simultaneously contributed to the scrutiny he faced from other members of American society, specifically in the context of gender. In one of the earliest critical looks into Sinatra's wartime career, E. J. Kahn Jr. mentions one critic, who

> expressed the opinion that Sinatra's singing "conforms to the usual crooning standards—each phrase begun slightly behind the beat, with soft, insinuating scoops and slides between the notes, and a dropping away of the voice after every line," [and] felt impelled to add a postscript to the effect that "a friend of mine who thinks much about these things finds this style very dangerous to our morale, for it is passive, luxurious, and ends up not with a bang but a whimper."[29]

Multiple scholars have explored the complex way in which male singers and crooning in the first half of the twentieth century fit within American fears and ideas regarding gender expression. Allison McCracken's work on this subject, for example, addresses the way Rudy Vallée's performance style shifted from one of relatively widespread popularity to one that was deemed effeminate and threatening to American gender ideals in the context of the Great Depression. McCracken then highlights how the celebrity persona of Bing Crosby, which aligned more closely with American codes of masculinity, was able to paint the image of crooners in a more positive light among both American men and women starting in the late 1930s.[30] Crosby was able to maintain this mainstream image of the seemingly all-American man throughout the duration of his career.

Freya Jarman-Ivens has also contributed to the dialogue regarding Crosby's image as an acceptably masculine crooner, stemming from McCracken's work. Jarman-Ivens suggests, however, that Sinatra's crooner persona aligned with Crosby's in this way, suggesting that "Sinatra's 'stylish virility' was a further move towards reassuring audiences of the normative masculinity of the genre's [crooning] exponents."[31] While Sinatra did develop and

---

[29] E. J. Kahn Jr., *The Voice: The Story of an American Phenomenon* (New York: Harper & Brothers, 1946), 7.
[30] Allison McCracken, *Real Men Don't Sing: Crooning in American Culture* (Durham, NC: Duke University Press, 2015).
[31] Freya Jarman-Ivens, "'Don't Cry, Daddy': The Degeneration of Elvis Presley's Musical Masculinity," in *Oh Boy!: Masculinities and Popular Music*, ed. Freya Jarman-Ivens (New York: Routledge, 2007), 174–175.

maintain a celebrity persona defined by codes of masculinity from the 1950s on, as Chapter 5 addresses, claiming that Sinatra demonstrated "normative masculinity" overlooks his initial performance persona in the 1940s, which was defined not by masculinity, but by a decidedly negative effeminacy in the eyes of many critics. Sinatra's persona and musicality during World War II in fact aligned much more closely with how female singers were generally viewed in contrast to male singers, namely in that he expressed vulnerability and "private emotions" in contrast to more public value-oriented male singers like Crosby.[32]

By examining Sinatra's particular vocal style, we can see how his musicality successfully translated this perceived intimacy to audiences. It is once again helpful to compare Sinatra to Crosby. As was discussed in the description of the 1945 *All Star Bond Rally* in Chapter 1, Crosby's singing style was characterized by a laid-back yet clear and strong baritone voice. In a sense, Crosby's vocality—along with his overall celebrity persona—was meant to seem representative of the average American person, rather than overly trained and florid.[33] Crosby's choice of songs, signature whistling, and easy "bub-bub-bub" scatting distinguished him from other more traditional crooners (such as Rudy Vallée) as well as jazz singers. While Crosby's vocal style was certainly not one that in reality was necessarily easy for any average person to replicate and demonstrated sophisticated techniques, the fact that he was able to deliver his musicality in a way that on the surface seemed accessible to the average person solidified his popularity among American men and women of all ages.

In analyzing Sinatra's musical traits, many critics and scholars have dismissed his vocality in the 1940s, suggesting that it lacked the maturity and nuance of his later vocal style. Roger Gilbert, for example, writes:

> Interestingly in his earliest phase, during the early and mid-'40s, Sinatra's vocal style is much closer to Crosby's than it would eventually become. While the young Sinatra's voice is thinner and reedier, his effortless, smooth vocal production, legato phrasing, and relative lack of dynamics owe an obvious debt to Crosby. Only in the '50s, after a series of setbacks and vocal

---

[32] Lewis A. Erenberg, *Swingin' the Dream: Big Band Jazz and the Rebirth of American Culture* (Chicago: University of Chicago Press, 1998), 85.

[33] Paula Lockheart, "A History of Early Microphone Singing, 1925–1939: American Mainstream Popular Singing at the Advent of Electronic Microphone Amplification," *Popular Music and Society* 26, no. 3 (2003): 381–382.

problems, did Sinatra develop the percussive, emotionally fraught style that led to his greatest recordings.[34]

Upon closer listening, however, Sinatra's voice during the 1940s was markedly different from Crosby's, in that he often emphasized notes in higher registers, lagged behind and stretched beats, and utilized immense breath control to produce very long, smooth phrases. Sinatra additionally would bend pitches and slide between them, sometimes sliding nearly an octave at a time. Sinatra's performances in the 1940s also demonstrate significant dynamic range. One notable technique he demonstrated was increasing dynamics in higher registers, pushing to what sometimes sounded like the brink of cracking a note, then coming back down both in pitch and dynamic, resulting in dramatic tension and release both aurally and emotionally.

Sinatra's musical characteristics are exemplified in sections of fan club journals that included narrative re-enactments of hearing Sinatra live, a common feature that journal editors often requested from members so others who had not been able to see Sinatra in person could share in the experience. These re-enactments often emphasized the feeling of cultivating personal connections with Sinatra during his performances that fans experienced and yearned for. E. J. Kahn Jr.'s 1946 study of Sinatra's wartime career includes a fairly accurate description of the importance of these narrative re-enactments within Sinatra fan clubs:

> Most of Sinatra's fans are insatiable for information about him and find that the sustenance provided by movie magazines—articles with titles like "That Old Sinatra Magic," "Sweet Sinatra," and "Sinatra—Prophet of Peace?"—is, like chop suey, filling enough but of little nutritive value. Their fan-club publications, mostly mimeographed affairs, which deal exclusively, and often lengthily, with Sinatra, provide more nourishment. Nearly every issue contains sentimental poems and an account of a dream in which the author met the singer. (Any club member who does meet or even see him can be counted on for two thousand words about the experience.)[35]

Sinatra fan club journals did not only include material relating directly to Sinatra, as Kahn suggests (though Sinatra was of course the main topic

---

[34] Gilbert, "Beloved and Notorious," 179.
[35] Kahn, *The Voice*, 77.

of interest), but Kahn was correct in indicating the importance of club members sharing any experiences they may have had with Sinatra, whether it be attending a concert or seeing him on the street, with their fellow members. Being the devoted fans they were, most club members desired to see or hear Sinatra in person if given the chance and wanted to hear what it was like from their peers who were lucky enough to have that experience. As Esther Bergquist's letter suggests, however, fans also valued hearing about these experiences in part because they wanted to feel like they knew who the "real" Sinatra was and experience the intimate connections he was known for creating with audiences in performance.[36]

Sinatra's seemingly real personality and his actions outside of his performances were just as important to his fans, as addressed in Chapter 3, as his musicianship. And within his musical performances, fans greatly valued what they felt to be expressions of Sinatra's authentic self, in part because this worked to foster the feeling that they shared a legitimate connection with Sinatra when he sang. This was one reason fans were enthusiastic to read firsthand accounts of encounters with Sinatra from fellow fans. One account of seeing Sinatra in concert, by Sing with the Sinatras Club member Gloria Heiskanen, emphasized the way Sinatra seemed to make personal connections with individual audience members when performing:

> The spotlight flashed on the stage then the screams went up because everyone thought Frank would come out, but it was only the band ... then he came out and for the 1st time I saw him in person.
>   He kidded around for a while then he sang "It's Been A Long, Long Time," "Sweet Loraine," [sic] "Where or When," "All the Things You Are." He makes you feel like he were talking and singing to you only. He treats the audience as guests and you feel as if you had known him for years.... When we left the place we knew we would always adore Frank because he has everything anyone could hope for in a man. He's just for us. He will always have a special place in my heart ... my heart and a million other hearts. May he ever be KING.[37]

Sinatra was described frequently in fan texts as making individual audience members feel as if he was singing directly to them, a notable skill when

---

[36] Barbas, *Movie Crazy*, 162.
[37] Gloria Heiskanen, "My Most Unforgettable Experience," *T-Jacket Journal* (February–March 1946), 8, Rose MARBL.

considering that seeing Sinatra live usually meant audience members were packed in with hundreds of other fans.

Alongside descriptions of this intimate performance characteristic, fans also worked to replicate the actual sound and musicality of Sinatra's voice in their accounts of seeing him. One striking way that many club members achieved this was by writing out the lyrics of songs Sinatra sang in an exaggerated way that was supposed to be reflective of his phrasing and other vocal traits, such as sliding between pitches and bending pitches. We can see examples of this in two different issues of *Sinatra-ly Yours*, published by the Semper Sinatra's Fan Club. In the Fall 1944 issue, member Lois Brundage of Montclair, New Jersey, described her experience being in the audience of one of Sinatra's radio broadcasts. The account is lengthy, describing everything from her bus ride to the studio, to waiting in line, to finally seeing Sinatra perform. In reference to the performance, Brundage writes:

> Then, Frank, with due respect to any adults present, but obviously singing for "kids only" really slayed 'em all with "She's Funny That Way." The same old Frank that made them swoon from coast to coast, had us all gasping for breath as he murmured softly, "I'm not much to look at—nothing to see—glad that I'm living and sooo lucky to be-e-e I got a woman who's crazy for me—she's funny that-t-t wa-ay!" Applause was deafening—and of course Barbara and I clapped as hard as any one.[38]

In the Winter 1945 issue of the same journal, member Peggy McShane provides a similarly lengthy and detailed account of her experience traveling to and seeing Sinatra live at the Paramount in New York. An excerpt of her essay re-enacts Sinatra's performance with the same exaggerated-lyric technique:

> He walked masterfully across the stage, smiled a-la-Sinatra and promptly sang "There'll be a hot time in the town of Berliiiinnn." ... He was going to sing a medley of three songs next, he said smiling down at me. Oh, that floor was so cool. Of course, he was smiling at ME. Listen, I know when a person smiles at me and when they don't. The songs were "I Walk Alone." "Puhleeeeeee, walk aloooooone" (don't worry I will Frankie,

---

[38] Lois Brundage, "A Visit to Frank's Wednesday Night Show," *Sinatra-ly Yours* 1, no. 3 (Fall 1944): 6, Sinatra-ana.

we screamed) "Till you're walking beside meeeeeeee, puhleeeeese walk aloooooooone."

Everyone verbally assured him he needn't worry, and we went on to the next number. "Come Out, Wherever you Are." "Where are you deeeeaaaar?" (here I am Fuuraankie, waved every hand in the place) He waved back and went into "I Don't Know Why I Love You Like I Do," an old and sentimental love ballad. The rendition was truly good and swoony.[39]

While fans could of course listen to Sinatra themselves through radio and records even if they were not able to hear him in person, the fact that club members prioritized sharing actual experiences of seeing and hearing Sinatra live with as much detail as possible indicates that traditional reviews of Sinatra's performances from professional critics or fan magazines were not enough. Fans did desire to hear news of new recordings and broadcasts of Sinatra and were interested in reading reviews of them, but of more value to fans was using music criticism to create connections, both real and imaginary, with Sinatra, and perhaps more significantly, with their fellow fans.

Gender and Vulnerability in Sinatra Fan Clubs

While this study is primarily focused on the young female fans of Frank Sinatra—as the overwhelmingly majority of fan club members were female—it is important to acknowledge now the small group of male fans that participated in these clubs, particularly in the context of self-expression through creative club contributions, as well as participation by both males and females who may not have identified as heterosexual. While Sinatra was known colloquially as "The Voice," attention should also be given to the fact that his physicality proved to be an important factor in his appeal to audiences who may have desired power and freedom in their romantic and sexual relationships, even if this power had to be restricted to fantasy.

As has been touched on throughout this book, wartime expectations of American masculinity were centered on promoting images of both physical

---

[39] Peggy McShane, "I, a Bobby-Soxer—Or the Confessions of the Bobby-Sox Brigade," *Sinatra-ly Yours* 1, no. 4 (Winter 1945): 4–6, Sinatra-ana.

and emotional male strength on the home front and to the world.[40] For those men and teenage boys who did not adhere to mainstream standards of strength and heterosexuality, navigating a wartime society where these standards were at the forefront of propaganda and entertainment was exceptionally challenging, and many had no choice but to hide any feelings of vulnerability or fear they may have felt. Because Frank Sinatra served as a public male figure that did not hide expressions of vulnerability—despite widespread public criticism—some boys could look to him as an example and personification of their own feelings.

Additionally, World War II was a unique moment in the history of homosexuality in America. On the one hand, public displays and declarations of homosexuality for both men and women were taboo, yet on the other, military life proved to allow for more nuance in homosexual and homosocial relationships. Neil Miller suggests the United States' entry into World War II strengthened a formerly "weak sense of American gay and lesbian identity" through the mobilization and movement of young people from rural areas to urban and sex-segregated military environments.[41] Miller further explains how World War II marked the first time that the US military asked recruits about their sexuality, though unsurprisingly many lied in order to find acceptance both within the military and society in general.[42] Despite these regulations, the homosocial environment of the military resulted in a "buddy" culture that allowed for a variety of different kinds of male relationships out of necessity, some heterosexual, some homosexual, and some that were more fluid.[43]

The combination of relative flexibility regarding male relationships in the US military and the raw expressions of vulnerability and heartache Sinatra demonstrated during the war meant that some men and teenage boys— who unlike teenage girls were able to enlist in the military—both could relate to Sinatra and desire him in nuanced ways, just as teenage girls did. I will reiterate once again that most Sinatra fan club members were female, and Sinatra's absence in the military made him unpopular among many

---

[40] See Chapter 1 for a more detailed examination of how perceptions and expectations of American masculinity shifted from the Great Depression to World War II.
[41] Neil Miller, *Out of the Past: Gay and Lesbian History from 1869 to the Present* (New York: Vintage, 1995), 231.
[42] Miller, *Out of the Past*, 231–232.
[43] Allan Bérubé, *Coming Out under Fire: The History of Gay Men and Women in World War Two* (New York: Free Press, 1990), 37–38.

servicemen, but there are some notable instances of male participation and admiration in fan club journals.

In terms of female sexuality, acknowledgment of potential lesbian relationships during the war was even less common than those between gay males. This tendency to ignore homoeroticism between females is also addressed in studies of American girl fan cultures specifically, such as in the work of Barbara Jane Brickman, who notes that the idea of "girlhood" in Western culture has been desexualized, yet even so, this desexualization is presumed to be heterosexual, leaving the lesbian girl "doubly erased."[44] While it is generally not possible to confirm Sinatra club members' sexuality based on their fan club journals, the sympathetic, open, and respectful attitudes members shared with one another coupled with their mutual admiration of a star marked as effeminate and emotionally open allows space to consider that members could develop romantic feelings and relationships—both real and imagined—not only with Sinatra, but with their fellow club members as well.[45] Brickman makes this important point, presenting the possibility that "it is not just the boy but also the girl in the pop star who attracts the fan's desires. It is this same-sex desire for the star, within girlhood's 'bedroom culture' and between female fans, that the scholarship has too often neglected."[46]

The trust and understanding relationships Sinatra fan club members shared with each other and their desire toward Sinatra is especially evident in original member poetry, which was found in almost every issue of most journals. Like the narrative re-enactments of seeing Sinatra live, fan poems served multiple purposes, primarily acting as a way to comment on Sinatra's performance style while simultaneously expressing their adoration. One example of a poem written by a male club member was submitted to the Fall 1944 issue of *Sinatra-ly Yours*, by Semper Sinatra Fan Club member Dick Yates. The poem, titled, "Frankie—My Choice," notably reinforces the idea of Bing Crosby as a more masculine singer suited for both men and women:

---

[44] Barbara Jane Brickman, "This Charming Butch: The Male Pop Idol, Girl Fans, and Lesbian (in) Visibility," *Journal of Popular Music Studies* 28 (2016): 447.
[45] See Diana W. Anselmo, *A Queer Way of Feeling: Girl Fans and Personal Archives of Early Hollywood* (Oakland: University of California Press, 2023), for a fascinating in-depth study of how girls in the United States used their movie fandom to resist normative expectations of femininity and navigate queer feelings and relationships during the early twentieth century.
[46] Brickman, "This Charming Butch," 453.

> He makes them go round in whirls,
> Most boys are for Crosby, the old king of song.
> Everytime I hear him I go down with a dong.
> But the new king of song, sends me along,
> With the bobby sox whirl of today.
> He's my choice.⁴⁷

Another poem by a male member was included in the first edition of *Ora e Sempre Sinatra*, by a Pvt. John Martin, who was a member of multiple Sinatra fan clubs. His poem, titled "Our Idol," highlights those musical aspects of Sinatra that fans admired—such as his high register, long phrasing, and intimate connections with audience members—but also demonstrates emotional vulnerability:

> Sinatra is his name,
> And I'm nuts about the guy,
> I'm proud to make the claim,
> And here are the reasons why.
>
> I like the way he walks,
> As he comes out on the stage,
> And as he slowly talks,
> You know just why he's the rage.
>
> I like the way he stands,
> In front of a microphone,
> The way he holds his hands,
> As he sings to you alone.
>
> I like his crooked tie,
> And also his mussed up hair,
> The twinkle in his eye,
> And the way he seems to care.
>
> I like the voice that thrills,
> It does so much to my heart,

---

[47] Dick Yates, "Frankie—My Choice," *Sinatra-ly Yours* (Fall 1944), 3, Sinatra-ana.

> *It sort of gives me chills,*
> *And it knocks me all apart.*
>
> *I like those gentle sighs,*
> *That he puts into a song,*
> *The way his voice will rise,*
> *And can hold a note so long.*[48]

Pvt. Martin clearly felt comfortable sharing such personal sentiments with other club members, reiterating the unspoken judgment-free policy present in most clubs. This is also demonstrated by a short note from the editor after Martin's poem that reads, "Thank you John, we appreciate your wonderful effort."

Other poems by female members, which were much more common than those by male members, reflect similar sentiments surrounding the emotional responses fans had to Sinatra's performances. Two representative examples can be found in the May 1945 issue of *The Voices Echo*, published by the Our Guy Frankie Fan Club, and the Spring 1945 issue of the *BowTie Bugle*, published by the Society for Souls Suffering from Sinatritis. The first example, written by Lucille Manzi, reads:

> *Frankie is a special name*
> *Sinatra is a name of fame,*
> *He himself is a wonderful guy,*
> *And there are plenty of reasons why.*
>
> *His voice! Oh gosh, it's just the best*
> *It's better far than all the rest.*
> *He may not have Jon Hall's physique,*
> *But, then again, he's far from weak.*
>
> *His eyes are like the skies of June.*
> *But, there [sic] not all that make us swoon*
> *We love the curl that's in his hair.*
> *For his is one that's very rare.*

---

[48] Pvt. John Martin, "Our Idol," *Ora e Sempre Sinatra*, Edition 1 (c. Summer 1945), 2, author's collection.

> *These are few of the reasons why,*
> *We think of him as our guy.*[49]

The second example, written by Sophie Tsoule, expresses similar sentiments:

> *They say a song that's sung by Bing*
> *Is tops among those who can really sing,*
> *But what they say is really very wrong,*
> *For Frankie can solidly put over a song.*
>
> *But there are a few of the ladies,*
> *Marys, Margies, Ruths, and Sadies,*
> *Who really insist upon swooning,*
> *While Frankie is up there so sweetly crooning.*
>
> *He may be thin and as said undernourished,*
> *But he has willpower and also some courage,*
> *For how God builds you is what you take,*
> *So he cannot change himself for anyones [sic] sake.*
>
> *He is a top singer, A number 1,*
> *His voice is from heaven, strictly from over the sun,*
> *Just sit there and listen, give him a try,*
> *And shortly you will be heaving a mighty sigh!*[50]

Notable in both examples are the references to Sinatra's physical characteristics. Sinatra's physicality was used as a point of ridicule toward Sinatra from much of wartime society, as was described in Chapter 2. One journalist from the *New York Herald Times*, for example, described Sinatra as having an "ugly, bony face."[51] Another, from the *Atlanta Constitution*, wrote, "if this undersized, pleasantly homely kid is the reincarnation of Rudolph Valentino, Rudy Vallee, Bing Crosby and Charles Boyer, then I am Lana Turner in a bathing suit! What Frankie has got that the rest of you boys haven't got is

---

[49] Lucille Manzi, "Our Guy," *The Voices Echo* 1, no. 1 (May 1945): 4, Sinatra-ana.
[50] Sophie Tsoule, "Sighs for Sinatra," *BowTie Bugle*, no. 7 (c. Spring 1945): 5, Sinatra-ana.
[51] Howard Barnes, "Higher and Higher," *New York Herald Tribune*, January 22, 1944: 6.

Figure 4.2 Front cover of the *BowTie Bugle* (1945) drawn by Patty Culhane. Hoboken Historical Museum.

beyond me!"[52] Within his fan communities, though, Sinatra's appearance proved to be a significant factor in his fans' adoration of him and contributed to their overall experiences as audience members and their criticism of his performances.

Member poems like those above suggest that Sinatra's deviations from mainstream expectations of masculine bodies—namely, that he was considered scrawny and had an unruly haircut—was extremely attractive to his young fans. Fan club members often created illustrations of Sinatra for their journals (Figures 4.2 and 4.3) and descriptions of Sinatra's appearance can be found throughout. An excerpt from a poem written by Frankie's United Swooners member Bonnie Hammons for example, reads:

---

[52] Inez Robb, "Inez Robb Wonders What Frank Sinatra Has That Other Crooners Don't Have," *Atlanta Constitution*, July 11, 1943: 2.

Figure 4.3 Front cover of *The Voice* (1944) drawn by Betsy Wenninger. Hoboken Historical Museum.

> *We love your height, your weight and smile*
> *We love your tousled hair,*
> *We love your eyes, and those bow-ties*
> *And the sport clothes that you wear.*[53]

In addition to writing about Sinatra's appearance, fan club members coveted visual memorabilia of Sinatra, and often traded "snaps" (snapshots) of Sinatra in exchange for other Sinatra-themed objects such as recordings, newspaper clippings, or most commonly, other photographs. Sinatra's image was a valuable commodity in fan clubs and allowed club members to claim and adapt aspects of Sinatra's appearance (such as incorporating his floppy bowties into their own wardrobes) to suit their own desires.

---

[53] Bonnie Hammons, "Ode to Frank Sinatra," *The Sinatra Sender* 1, no. 3 (June 1945): 2, Sinatra-ana.

As Richard Dyer notes, "Pin-ups of white men are awkward things... they exemplify a set of dichotomies—they are pictures to be looked at, but it is not the male role to be looked at; they are passive objects of gaze, but men are supposed to be the active subjects of gaze, and so on."[54] This suggests that both commenting on Sinatra's appearance and also possessing visual representations of Sinatra's face and body in a way provided teenage girls with a sense of power: power to freely adore Sinatra and speak openly about his body within the safety of their clubs, while society expected them to maintain sexual innocence and mainstream characteristics of femininity. Claiming Sinatra's body for their own enjoyment was yet another way that teen girls deviated from what we might consider to be traditional music criticism, but contributed to a different form of criticism that reveals far more about their experiences and desires as wartime girls than a professional record or concert review could.

Moving beyond Sinatra, however, this fan criticism reveals something even more significant than just the fact that teen girls were actively expressing what they valued and enjoyed in popular music. That is, in an era when outward expressions of sentimentality, sexuality, and vulnerability—among both men and women—were generally discouraged in American society, teenage fans felt comfortable sharing personal feelings and expressions of adoration towards Sinatra with their fellow fans. The primary cause of public scorn toward Sinatra and his female audience during World War II was that he was eliciting what was deemed grossly inappropriate public displays of female hysteria and sexuality. In other words, teenage girls generally could not express their adoration of Sinatra in public without facing outrage or psychoanalytic criticism of such unnatural behavior. For those fans who felt a desire to express their adoration in tangible ways outside of their own minds and bodies, fan clubs and club journals provided organized vehicles for doing so where fan expressions of desire toward Sinatra were not only accepted, but highly valued by other fans.

Conclusion

Considering these textual artifacts of 1940s fan reception in the context of discourses in music criticism, we can once again look to Christopher Dingle's

---

[54] Richard Dyer, *Heavenly Bodies: Film Stars and Society* (New York: St. Marten's Press, 1986), 117.

introduction to *The Cambridge History of Music Criticism* to understand the role fan club journals and other fan-made objects can play in this discourse. Solidifying why scholars should consult music criticism to further our historical understandings of how music affects people's lived experiences, Dingle explains, "music criticism essentially supplies a continuous contemporaneous record of what was happening in music, and how it was viewed by some. Far from a fatal flaw, its generally unguarded lack of consideration is often the prime value of music criticism. Moreover, music criticism frequently provides the only record of what actually happened and even how it sounded."[55] Of course, being a performer in an age of recording, broadcasting, film, and mass-produced print media, the texts created by fans of Frank Sinatra are not the only record of Sinatra's wartime career. However, these texts are the only record of how Sinatra was received by teenage girls from their own perspectives.

Viewing these fan texts as a form of music criticism serves as a model for how scholars can carve out new narratives in music history that include the perspectives of social groups that currently lie in the periphery of music history's dominant narrative. In the case of Sinatra's teenage fans, their unique forms of music criticism reveal components of their "horizons of expectations," which can be used to answer certain historical questions, particularly why their fan communities were so important and what they got out of them. We see that these communities not only prioritized high quality and nuanced performances, but also the cultivation of real and imagined relationships with celebrities and each other through these performances.

---

[55] Dingle, "Introduction," 2.

5

Postwar Changes

A New Sinatra and the Decline of the Bobbysoxers

President Truman tonight proclaimed Sunday, Sept. 2, as VJ-Day—for Japan a day of "retribution," for America and the world a day of the "victory of liberty over tyranny."
—"Truman Victory Speech Proclaims Today VJ-Day,"
Los Angeles Times, September 2, 1945

The tumult and the shouting may have died down a bit, but Boston still was in a victory mood last night, and kept right on whooping up the Japanese surrender in high-caliber style....

The crowds were there, the bottles were still plentiful, the girls were still being kissed, and bars and night clubs still were jammed.
—"Boston Keeps Up Victory Whoopee,"
Daily Boston Globe, August 16, 1945

When Germany confirmed its unconditional surrender to the Allied nations on May 8, 1945, followed by Japan's surrender on August 15, 1945, the United States felt a collective sense of relief and celebration. The war was over. American servicemen would be coming home. Americans could begin rebuilding their lives and try to move on. American media published messages and images that expressed national attitudes of both solemnity and frivolity, feelings that Americans understandably moved between at the war's end.

The United States' postwar recovery was of course not as simple as going back to what was "normal" in the years preceding World War II. Too much had changed. Not only had thousands of Americans lost loved ones, but society went through incredibly drastic changes that would permanently influence the direction of the nation. Many women who did not work before the war were now used to doing so. African Americans and other minorities were able—to an extent—to move past the domestic and unskilled working roles they were previously limited to into more skilled roles. American servicemen had faced incredibly stressful and traumatic experiences. As relieved as the United States felt at the war's end, it quickly became clear that things would not go back to "normal," and that society would have to face some serious questions and challenges in building postwar life.

For American women and teenage girls in particular, the contradictory messaging regarding postwar expectations was overwhelming. Women who had taken on jobs were unsure if they should give them up to returning servicemen, or if they should continue to pursue careers. Black and working-class women who needed to work feared being pushed back into the limited employment roles they were restricted to before the war. And teenage girls who were entering adulthood, in many cases without much work experience, had to decide whether they would pursue careers or a primarily domestic lifestyle. Complicating all of this was a new nationwide emphasis on seemingly ideal suburban futures, in which female domesticity and national conformity were advertised as the ultimate key to postwar happiness. Many Americans did strive for these suburban lifestyles, but others felt restricted in such a future. And for many minorities and working-class Americans, this kind of future would not be available even to those who desired it.

Mass media and popular culture also shifted in the years immediately following World War II, with increasing emphasis on the booming consumer market and popular culture figures who demonstrated postwar ideals of whiteness, national pride, and mainstream values. Bing Crosby is an example of the type of celebrity who maintained success in the postwar years, largely by exhibiting these characteristics.

Frank Sinatra, on the other hand, experienced a dramatic celebrity transformation in the years following the war into the 1950s, fueled in part by challenges in his personal life. For the teenage female members of Frank Sinatra fan clubs—who as we have seen throughout this book demonstrated wide and varied interests, desires, and ideas regarding both their personal futures and that of their communities—Sinatra's persona was no longer the one they admired so greatly during World War II. It was no longer the persona created specifically for them. This is not to say that all of Sinatra's wartime fans were suddenly no longer fans of him—indeed, many continued to support the singer through the remainder of his career—but as the bobbysoxers began entering adulthood and navigating postwar gender, class, and race dynamics, their identification with Sinatra lessened.

Through examining the changing postwar climate of gender, youth, and overall social experiences of American citizens—influenced in part by increasing Cold War anxieties—this chapter will explore how American teenage girls, and specifically the wartime fans of Frank Sinatra, made the transition from bobbysoxers to young adults building their postwar lives. Key to this examination is understanding not just the personal and celebrity changes Sinatra experienced during this time, but how his shifting persona reflected widespread postwar perceptions of American vulnerability, anxiety, and masculinity. Through considering fan responses to Sinatra's very public separation from his first wife and ensuing romantic affairs, his musical career challenges, and his generally unacknowledged performance in the 1952 film *Meet Danny Wilson*, we can see how Sinatra and his former bobbysoxer admirers provide a specific and revealing perspective on American postwar culture.

Postwar Women

One of the biggest questions facing American women at the end of World War II was what their futures may hold as working citizens. Thousands of women who had not worked before the start of the war experienced new opportunities, fulfillment, and financial independence. Women from working-class backgrounds who had worked before the war were, in many cases, able to branch out into roles previously closed to them. But would all of that continue now that the war was over? Mass media and government messaging did not provide clear answers to this question, and newspapers published articles both in support of and objection to women remaining in the workforce.

One article in a 1947 edition of the *Chicago Defender*—notably authored by a woman—made the case that many American women were working even before World War II and should be encouraged to continue:

> Women have always worked, although usually without the glamour attributed to war-time "Rosie the Riveter." . . . Women work because they have to, yet, when they look for work today, they are met with age restrictions, demands for more highly developed skills, or are placed at the

bottom of the economic ladder, with substandard wages.... In addition to the role of wife, mother, homemaker, women often must be responsible for family support and financial maintenance of the home.[1]

The article goes on to address the need for equal pay for women and the fact that many women were not working out of selfishness, as some believed, but out of necessity to support their families. In many cases, this included injured or disabled servicemen returning from the war.

While many media outlets published material in support of women working postwar, many others did not. One 1946 edition of the *Daily Boston Globe* included a reader write-in, who was clearly of the opinion that American women should have returned home at the war's end:

> To the Editor—I am one of the 53,000 ablebodied but unemployed veterans of Massachusetts....
>
> I have scanned the Globe's employment column and have made the rounds day after day for the past six weeks in search of employment, but alas, my search up to now has been fruitless. Why? Because, as I have found and the newspaper's employment section reveals, the big demand is for women. The employers, in their quest for cheap labor, are completely disregarding the fact that the backbone of this great country is the family, and that in our society the man is supposed to be the breadwinner.
>
> Veterans and nonveterans alike are being deprived of the means of supporting their families simply because the labor market is flooded with women who have no one to support but the makers of cosmetics. Did we fight for "freedom from want"? If so, we haven't won yet.[2]

Although servicemen understandably faced significant and real challenges when they returned from war—including trouble reassimilating to civilian life, post-traumatic stress disorder, and as this reader indicates, finding employment—this reader's dismissal of the fact that thousands of American women were working out of necessity and professional fulfillment and not simply to support "the makers of cosmetics" was reflective of widespread beliefs that further inhibited women's abilities and confidence to pursue work. But despite the contradictory expectations and messages

---

[1] Rebecca Stiles Taylor, "Women Always Worked, 'Rosie the Riveter' Added Glamour to Fact," *Chicago Defender*, March 22, 1947, 17.
[2] "More Jobs for Women, than for Veterans," *Daily Boston Globe*, February 23, 1946, 14.

spread regarding women's employment in the postwar years, women did in fact continue to have an increasing presence in the immediate postwar workforce.[3] This fact did not, however, overshadow the new nationwide emphasis on pursuit of postwar domesticity and suburban lifestyles.

Popular memory tends to imagine the late 1940s and 1950s in America as a time of newfound affluence, consumerism, and suburban life. Indeed, after experiencing the trauma and lack of resources of World War II, many Americans dreamed of a new kind of life in which suburban homeownership, disposable income, and an emphasis on nuclear families could be their reality. This imagined ideal, however, was not a product solely of wartime lack and family separation. Growing anxieties surrounding communism and the Cold War further contributed to a national emphasis on conforming to an American image that was marked as decidedly different from Soviet counterparts.

John Fousek explains how in the initial period following America's victory in World War II, the nation felt a responsibility to set an example for the rest of the world of economic prosperity, moral values, and overall global unity. This feeling was short-lived, however, because as Fousek notes, tensions between the United States and the Soviet Union led to images of a divided world in contrast to "the idea of One World united around American values."[4] The United States responded to the perceived threat to American values by leaning heavily into mainstream, white American ideals, key among these being the nuclear family. As Sherrie Tucker writes, "More than a lifestyle, the nuclear family expressed an ideology of cocoonlike conformity and was variously credited with protecting the American way of life against nuclear threat, Communist takeover, the plotting of subversives to undermine the U.S.-controlled international capitalist system, and a postwar reprise of the Great Depression."[5] While this lifestyle appeared to many Americans to be the key to achieving and maintaining postwar happiness and distinction from Cold War enemies, the fact was that this lifestyle was restricted only to those Americans who aligned with the national image the United States hoped to display to the rest of the world. That image was one of affluence and whiteness.

---

[3] Sherrie Tucker, *Swing Shift: "All-Girl" Bands of the 1940s* (Durham, NC: Duke University Press, 2001), 317.

[4] John Fousek, *To Lead the Free World: American Nationalism & the Cultural Roots of the Cold War* (Chapel Hill: University of North Carolina Press, 2000), 188–189.

[5] Tucker, *Swing Shift*, 318.

For Americans who did not have the economic means or expected ethnicity, the postwar suburban dream was often out of reach. For women especially, coming from non-white and/or working-class backgrounds came with significant barriers in terms of pursuing suburban life, skilled working roles, or both. Subject to postwar "last hired, first fired" patterns, black women were often forced to move back into the kinds of domestic service roles they were limited to before World War II.[6] And the suburban lifestyle that was supposed to reflect ideal American values and nationwide conformity largely excluded black women, instead enforcing white standards of beauty, family, and assimilation.[7]

Where did all of these pressures and contradictions leave Americans who did not conform to these standards? And more specifically, for the purpose of this study, where did this leave American teenage girls who were entering adulthood in the postwar years and may have envisioned different futures for themselves? Answers to this were complex and confusing for many teenage girls, as they witnessed a female work revolution during the war years followed by a boom in consumer marketing used to encourage young women and teens to develop the skills needed to pursue primarily domestic roles. Just as in the years of World War II, however, the challenges teenage girls and young women faced in the postwar years did not mean they automatically became compliant. The different ways female youth engaged with postwar society were more nuanced than that, and American women and teenage girls continued to move the trajectory of changes in women's experiences in postwar America, although in different and often more subtle ways than how history tends to remember the women of World War II.

Postwar Teenage Girls

Arguably one of the most defining artifacts of American teenage girl culture—starting in the 1940s and continuing to this day—is *Seventeen* magazine. While entertainment magazines, and especially commercial fan magazines, had been targeted toward young women and teenage girls beginning earlier in the twentieth century, *Seventeen*, first published in 1944, was one of the first magazines dedicated specifically to covering the culture and desires of

---

[6] Tucker, *Swing Shift*, 318–319.
[7] Winie Breines, *Young, White, and Miserable: Growing Up Female in the Fifties* (Boston: Beacon, 1992), 15.

teenage girls. While driven by consumer marketing, *Seventeen* attempted to treat and portray American teenage girls not as mindless, entertainment-obsessed buyers, but as interested citizens. Kelly Schrum writes of *Seventeen*'s goals in the 1940s, "At the same time the magazine depended on advertisers' belief in the reliability of teenage girls as a unified market, it strove to combat negative stereotypes of swooning bobby-soxers" by sending the message that "the teenage girl cared about her world and would one day be a responsible citizen and therefore a responsible consumer."[8] This goal aligns with much of the media—both commercial and audience-made—this book has examined in the context of World War II. When the war ended, however, and American life began to reshape into the consumerist, suburban-driven system it would become in the 1950s, *Seventeen* magazine reshaped with it.

This is not to say that *Seventeen* suddenly dismissed teenage girls as mindless consumers destined for only one possible future. The magazine continued, and still continues, to publish content that catered to a variety of teenage interests in addition to entertainment and product coverage. The magazine, however, in part began to contribute to the contradictory messaging teenage girls were receiving in the immediate postwar years about what their options would be as they entered adulthood, and who exactly would be able to benefit from these options.

While *Seventeen*'s content during the final years of World War II emphasized how teenage girls could support the war effort—through buying war bonds, rationing, and so forth—the magazine shifted focus shortly after the war to increased spending (although the magazine still tried to send messages of responsible consumerism to some extent) and lessons in domesticity.[9] As Grace Palladino notes in reference to *Seventeen*'s postwar content, "Each month, the magazine offered mini-courses in home economics, complete with recipes, party plans, and decorating ideas by the dozen—and notes on where teenagers could buy the products they needed to put these plans into action."[10] This new emphasis on spending and home life of course reflected the same emphasis in society at large. As noted above, however, this lifestyle was not advertised to or achievable for all teenage girls, as *Seventeen*'s readership was mostly composed of white middle- and upper-middle-class

---

[8] Kelly Schrum, "'Teena Means Business': Teenage Girls' Culture and 'Seventeen' Magazine, 1944–1950," in *Delinquents & Debutantes: Twentieth-Century American Girls' Cultures*, ed. Sherrie A. Inness (New York: New York University Press, 1998), 143.
[9] Schrum, "'Teena Means Business,'" 155.
[10] Grace Palladino, *Teenagers: An American History* (New York: Basic Books, 1996), 103.

girls.[11] As with the Frank Sinatra fan communities featured throughout this study, it is hard to know exactly how heterogeneous *Seventeen*'s readership really was, even if the magazine attempted to reinforce nationwide messaging of America as an accepting melting pot when compared to the Soviet Union, which as has already been discussed, was not the reality. Just as with the war-era teenage girls we have seen, however, it is not so easy or accurate to assume that postwar teens and young women were the passive, nonresistant citizens that American society may have hoped they would be at the war's end.

In the midst of media images touting the ideal white, prosperous, suburban lifestyle of postwar America, there was another widespread commonality among American citizens that was growing increasingly prominent, that is, national feelings of fear, anxiety, and discontent as the Cold War established itself and Americans worked to rebuild their lives after the trauma of World War II. Wini Breines's work on white American female youth during this time sheds light on how teenage girls and young women experienced the postwar years and how they worked to shape their lives into ones that felt meaningful under immense pressure to conform. Breines describes how many white youth, primarily those who came from families that were able to afford the consumer-based postwar suburban life, felt trapped by what felt like a false sense of reality in their lifestyles and longed to express authentic individuality.[12] While many American teenage girls and young women may have been experiencing these feelings of discontent, however, this does not necessarily mean they were helpless in working toward creating more meaningful experiences in their own lives and their communities. The Frank Sinatra fan club members of World War II, for example, demonstrated that young American women and teens truly desired to discuss and take action on issues such as race and internationalism, and develop professional skills. That desire would not just disappear after the war's end. And as difficult as it was for these girls to navigate an entirely new set of pressures and expectations after the war, their desires would prove to continue affecting the directions America would take in decades to follow, even if these efforts were somewhat slowed by 1950s culture.

Breines makes this important point, noting, "their [young women's] restlessness was significant; they were laying the groundwork for rebellion in

---

[11] Schrum, "'Teena Means Business,'" 139.

[12] Wini Breines, "The 'Other' Fifties: Beats and Bad Girls," in *Not June Cleaver: Women and Gender in Postwar America, 1945–1960*, ed. Joanne Meyerowitz (Philadelphia: Temple University Press, 1994), 390.

the years ahead. In many cases, early nonconformists pioneered the social movements of the 1960s—civil rights workers, campus activists, and youthful founders of the women's liberation movement of the late 1960s."[13] This is not to say that all war-era teenage girls, and more specifically the teenage fans of Frank Sinatra, adopted mindsets of rebellion in their postwar lives. Many went on to embrace postwar suburban life and/or take on working roles that supported this life. What is important to remember, however, is that American women and youth did not simply experience a passive halt in progress during the 1950s. Rather, progress toward women's expansion in American society continued throughout the decade, if in a less visible way than in the surrounding decades of the 1940s and 1960s.[14]

For the wartime female fans of Frank Sinatra specifically, who had already begun to develop professional skills within their fan communities and view themselves as active citizens, the immediate postwar years also felt different because their idol was undergoing dramatic shifts in his celebrity persona, which some fans embraced and others rejected. In the late 1940s into the early 1950s, Sinatra transformed into a celebrity who challenged the notion of postwar American prosperity and domestic bliss, instead reflecting the less visible postwar feelings of anxiety and vulnerability. This transformation caused a divide in his former bobbysoxer fans between those who placed great value on pursuing mainstream American family life and those who identified more with the personal difficulties Sinatra faced after the war. Sinatra's fan base did not change overnight, of course. Instead, the immediate postwar years set the stage for a more nuanced transition for Sinatra from wartime idol of bobbysoxers to symbol of postwar adult sentimentality and vulnerability.

Postwar Sinatra

The immediate postwar years were not easy for Frank Sinatra. After a wartime skyrocket to fame, things came crashing down around him, both in his professional and personal life. The struggles appeared to begin around 1946 with rumors of Sinatra pursuing extramarital affairs. Although he and his first wife, Nancy Barbato, did not officially divorce until 1951, their increasing relationship problems were public knowledge throughout the latter half of the

---

[13] Breines, "The 'Other' Fifties," 383.
[14] Joanne Meyerowitz, "Introduction," in *Not June Cleaver*, ed. Meyerowitz, 4.

1940s, and were an initial catalyst in Sinatra's transition away from being a teen idol.

Evidence of the negative reactions many of Sinatra's wartime fans as well as their parents had toward the reports of Sinatra's deviance from mainstream marital values can be found in reader write-ins to entertainment media. Gossip columnist Hedda Hopper, for example, received multiple letters from her readers expressing their disdain for Sinatra's behavior. One letter from "The Bucknam Girls," who claimed Sinatra as their former idol, reads,

> Dear Hedda Hopper:
> We are incensed about the way our idol, Frank Sinatra, has acted. If it is true we hereby swear to <u>avoid</u> playing Frankie's records whenever they are requested, for we are members of Bucknam's San Diego Wired Music Co.
> Until we hear to the contrary we have changed Frankie's name to Frankie Not-So-Hot-Tra.[15]

Not all letters to Hopper were this concise. Another letter from "A Reader of the Times" attacks not only Sinatra, but his alleged extramarital love interest, Lana Turner:

> I used to listen to [Sinatra] because I thought he was different from the rest of that trash in Hollywood but now I am burned up!
> Lana Turner must be proud of herself to break up a nice little family like the Sinatra's [sic]. The public should boycott all the pictures of girls like her, it is a fine example to set for the younger people.
> I hope the bobbysoxers will stick together and put him on the skids it would do him good, it was the kids who made him, the older people couldn't stand him, at least every one I knew felt that way about him.
> All that Ballyho about him being such a wonderful husband and father makes me sick.... He ought to know Lana Turner will grab the next pair of pants that goes by. Marriage vows mean nothing to people like her, in my estimation it is just glorified legal prostitution. I am sick and tired of the whole mess, and anybody who pays money to see trash like that is a fool, they are no better than common street walkers.... Those girls make me think of a bunch of dogs in heat.[16]

---

[15] "The Bucknam Girls" to Hedda Hopper, October 18, 1946, Hedda Hopper papers, Margaret Herrick Library, Academy of Motion Pictures Arts and Sciences, Beverly Hills, CA (hereafter cited as Hedda Hopper papers).

[16] "A Reader of the Times" to Hedda Hopper, October 25, 1946, Hedda Hopper papers.

The negative reactions in letters such as these tended to focus on the fact that Sinatra betrayed marriage and family life, a mainstream nationwide priority during World War II, but especially in the postwar years. For those fans who pursued the path of the American ideal in the late 1940s and 1950s, Sinatra's infidelity challenged this path, in turn isolating those former fans who valued marriage and family above all else in their own lives.

Not all war-era Sinatra fans automatically condemned him, however. In response to the same article Hopper wrote that stoked the fierce criticism above, others wrote in defense of Sinatra and suggested his situation was not so black and white, while others showed more disappointment than criticism. One letter to Hopper from Jean Ellen Herdman is more critical of Hopper's reporting than Sinatra's actions:

> Dear Miss Hopper,
> I have been a loyal fan of Frank Sinatra's for a long time, and I feel sure I shall continue to be one for a long time to come.
> Since the separation of Frank and Nancy, you have written in your column, things which I believe have wronged Frank. I sincerely believe it takes two to break up a marriage—especially one that has lasted seven and one half years.
> Your unfair remarks reached a climax with todays [sic] (Oct 17) column. How can you insinuate that Frank desires to be free of his children? ...
> You say perhaps he will lose some of his fans. It seems as if you really do wish him too [sic]. I will admit writing such as was in your column would turn the more shallow people away from him. Any fan that really loved and admired Frank would not desert him now.
> Really, Miss Hopper, I cease to have any respect left for you at all.[17]

Another letter from a group of Sinatra fans notes that they feel a responsibility to let Hopper know how some of the "young people" feel about Sinatra's situation:

> We have a terrible let-down feeling to find our idol has feet of clay—we have felt all along that Frankie and his family were sort of our special property....
> What really troubles us is that maybe he just does not care about us anymore, now that he is so successful—for how can he go on making talks to us

---

[17] Jean Ellen Herdman to Hedda Hopper, October 17, 1946, Hedda Hopper papers.

on "Intolerance" and "Delinquency" etc. when he is really being delinquent himself?[18]

This letter is significant, because it solidifies the fact that Sinatra's young wartime fans felt they shared a genuine connection with the star and believed that he in turn felt the same way about them. This letter suggests Sinatra was unfaithful not just to his wife, but his entire fan base.

These few letters reflect the postwar divide in American life, with an almost aggressive emphasis on mainstream values of domesticity on one side, and an underlying sense of anxiety and discontent on the other. While Sinatra did alienate some of his former fans who disapproved of his lifestyle and image change, he simultaneously was able to identify with a whole new demographic of Americans after the war who were experiencing their own personal fears and uncertainties in the Cold War era. Sinatra's ability to reinvent himself around 1953 after losing "his recording contract, his film contract, his booking agency, and even his voice one night during a performance, due to a throat hemorrhage" was a near miraculous feat considering the extreme changes in Americans' lives as they left one global crisis and entered another.[19] Sinatra achieved this not by adhering to postwar conformity, but by unapologetically displaying vulnerability just as he did during World War II. But while Sinatra's wartime vulnerability was defined by sentimentality, longing, and an association with femininity, the vulnerability he displayed in the late 1940s and 1950s was instead reflective of shifts in American male identity and vulnerability.

Many have credited Sinatra's renewed success as well as his now famous ability to express the discontented and vulnerable side of Cold War American identity with his Academy Award–winning performance in *From Here to Eternity* (Columbia Pictures, 1953). Sinatra was praised for portraying Angelo Maggio, a character that became almost synonymous with Sinatra as an Italian American character who demonstrated difficulty in coping with the stresses of World War II military life and his own personal life. Sinatra did not serve in the military during World War II, but his public postwar career and personal fall was seen to be reflected in the character of Maggio. This was a turning point for Sinatra's career, because rather than once again facing

---

[18] S.T.F. to Hedda Hopper, October 13, 1946, Hedda Hopper papers.
[19] Keir Keightley, "Frank Sinatra, Hi-Fi, and Formations of Adult Culture: Gender, Technology, and Celebrity, 1948–62," PhD diss., Concordia University, 1996, 141.

criticism for portraying a vulnerable personality, he was now celebrated for his raw and relatable performance of an American man facing difficulty in coping with his war-defined life.

Sinatra's performance in *From Here to Eternity* occurred on the heels of his public whirlwind romance, marriage, and divorce from Ava Gardner, all of which occurred in the span of a few years. But just as with his role in *From Here to Eternity*, Sinatra was not necessarily condemned for this apparent desecration of American family values in the same way he was shortly after the war. Rather, as Keir Keightley describes, the reporting on Sinatra and Gardner's relationship "showed subtle shifts in attitudes toward Sinatra."[20] Keightley attributes this shift to a new, adult-based respect for Sinatra as someone who was no longer just a teen idol, but someone who had truly experienced personal hardship and was able to pull himself back up from it. The transition from Sinatra being seen as a celebrity for youth to one who was now more relatable to adults was key to his comeback and subsequent success. Keightley explains this transition further:

> Regardless of how long or hard a teen-identified performer might have worked for success, the gendered aspects of teen-idolhood encourage dismissal and resentment of what is seen as unmerited or manufactured popularity. Conversely, the very fact of his fall from the top of the heap in the late 1940s, and his subsequent come-back, imbued the Capitol Sinatra with a sense of experience, of a life lived through ups and downs, more intense than most, which would be hard to believe in a performer who simply rose to the top and stayed there; in other words, the history of Sinatra's career itself becomes a key component of his image ca. 1953–62.[21]

While Keightley and others are correct in crediting the early 1950s, and particularly 1953, as the key turning point in Sinatra's career, in large part due to *From Here to Eternity*, one of Sinatra's most forgotten film performances, which came out one year before *From Here to Eternity*, already demonstrated the postwar vulnerability and male anxiety he would be praised for displaying one year later.

---

[20] Keightley, "Frank Sinatra, Hi-Fi, and Formations of Adult Culture," 176.
[21] Keightley, "Frank Sinatra, Hi-Fi, and Formations of Adult Culture," 166.

Case Study: *Meet Danny Wilson*

Sinatra's 1952 film *Meet Danny Wilson* (Universal Pictures, 1952), although a flop at the time of its release, was the first of Sinatra's film performances to portray him as something other than the moral, shy, and somewhat effeminate character he typically played in his 1940s films, such as *Higher and Higher* (RKO, 1944), *Anchors Aweigh* (MGM, 1945), and *On the Town* (MGM, 1949). The film has been largely forgotten within Sinatra's exceedingly long and varied career history, in part because it was overshadowed by his Academy Award–winning performance in *From Here to Eternity* the following year. *Meet Danny Wilson* is a revealing artifact, however, not only of Sinatra's tumultuous postwar shift in celebrity persona, but of nationwide postwar shifts in experiences of American masculinity.

In an article from the *Los Angeles Times* dated shortly after the premiere of *Meet Danny Wilson*, critic Philip K. Scheuer takes issue with the contrast of Danny Wilson's character with Sinatra's own, or at least his previously perceived personality from the mid-1940s, writing:

> Frank Sinatra is obviously unfair to himself in "Meet Danny Wilson." For Danny's rise to fame and fortune as crooner and bobby-sox idol is so much like Frankie's that the parallel is inescapable. However, once he becomes a success Danny begins behaving in a manner decidedly not commensurate with the code of a gentleman. . . . Now, all these reactions are so palpably foreign to Frankie's own sweet nature that we hate to see him giving vent to them, even as Danny.[22]

As has been discussed, Sinatra had in fact already begun to show public signs of a changing celebrity persona as soon as 1946. This 1952 review, however, makes clear that while other areas of Sinatra's persona had already experienced extreme flux, the public was still used to specific types of film performances by Sinatra. Despite the increasingly widespread rumors of extramarital affairs, fights, and supposed mob associations that were already being published in the late 1940s, the moviegoing public was still able to see representations of the original idol of the bobbysoxers as late as 1949 in *On the Town*. Sinatra's character shift in *Meet Danny Wilson* was in a way the nail in the coffin of Sinatra's former war-era persona.

---

[22] Philip K. Scheuer, "Sinatra Plays Danny Wilson, Heel and Hero," *Los Angeles Times*, February 8, 1952, B7.

POSTWAR CHANGES   143

The film follows the career of singer Danny Wilson (Frank Sinatra) and his friend/accompanist Mike Ryan (Alex Nicol), two World War II veterans who are struggling to make ends meet after the war. The pair gets their big break when the main love interest of both men, Joy Carroll (Shelley Winters), hears them perform and offers them a spot at the club she is employed at. The successful club's mobster owner, Nick Driscoll (Raymond Burr), is romantically interested in Carroll, making it easy for her to convince him to give Wilson and Ryan a steady job at his club. There's a catch, however; Wilson must agree to give Driscoll 50 percent of his earnings for the rest of his life in exchange for helping Wilson become a star. Wilson agrees. The film then proceeds to portray Wilson's rise to stardom, becoming an object of adoration for thousands of young girls, only to see his romantic life with Carroll as well as his career take a downturn.

The film's plot was an obvious reflection of Sinatra's actual life and career up to this point. What audiences had not yet seen on film (though may have seen in media coverage) from Sinatra that they saw in Danny Wilson, however, was how Wilson handles these challenges. We see Wilson getting into fights, drinking excessively, and becoming violently entangled in mob dealings when he attempts to break his agreement with Nick Driscoll. In the end, Wilson is redeemed by saving Ryan's life and accepting Carroll's true preference for Ryan instead of himself.

The connection with Sinatra's life postwar and beyond is again obvious, as the remainder of his career always included rumors of mob associations and sometimes violent behavior, though those closest to him publicly defended Sinatra as a true friend and misunderstood person. But this period in Sinatra's life was still new to the film's 1952 audience. Despite this, the drastic change in Sinatra's screen image proved crucial to achieving the level of success he would find shortly after *Meet Danny Wilson* was made. Because while *Meet Danny Wilson* became a rather insignificant dot on the map of Sinatra's overall career, the characteristics he portrayed in the film not only won him an Oscar the very next year, but also came to define him for the rest of his life. The film also demonstrated a shift from Sinatra as a sweet, singing, and lovable film personality to one who was capable of "serious" acting, a shift that is generally credited to *From Here to Eternity*, as in the work of Keightley:

> Sinatra ... was in 1953 entering a second phase of his film career, in which he would be seen as a serious, dramatic actor. The prestige associated with Sinatra the dramatic Actor, appearing in "adult" films, and Sinatra the

singer of standards, together with his increased association with an adult audience (especially in nightclubs), would together mark his difference from teen culture and contribute to new conceptions of popular performers in the 1950s and later.[23]

Keightley's mention of Sinatra's shift in musical identity from that of a crooner to a self-proclaimed "saloon singer" is relevant to consider in the context of both *Meet Danny Wilson* and Sinatra's career shift in general because, again, this shift marked Sinatra as a celebrity associated more with adult audiences than with teens.

We see and hear Sinatra's new musicality in *Meet Danny Wilson*, even as he is simultaneously acting the part of teen idol, which audiences would have associated with his World War II–era performance style. At one point in the film, during the peak of Wilson's newfound success, Wilson performs "All of Me." This performance takes place in front of an audience of truly hysterical young girls who scream and sigh at Wilson's every movement and inflection. This audience again demonstrates an obvious parallel to Sinatra's own career, but the style of singing we hear as well as Danny Wilson's performance mannerisms are quite different from what Sinatra exhibited in the early to mid-1940s in his live performances for the bobbysoxers.

As described in Chapter 4, Sinatra's war-era voice was characterized by lyrical phrasing, creating feelings of intimacy with audience members, and exceptional breath control. Sinatra claimed to have learned breathing techniques from trombonist Tommy Dorsey while singing in his band, and Sinatra's impressively long phrases because of his skillful breathing became one of his musical signatures that set him apart from other singers. This in turn contributed to Sinatra's stylistic tendency to hold phrases for long durations, letting them end naturally rather than clipping them or ending them with hard stops in the throat or mouth. This is apparent in most of Sinatra's films of the 1940s. In terms of bodily mannerisms while performing, Sinatra was notably subdued during his live performances during World War II, refraining from such gestures as snapping, clapping, stomping, or even straying too far from his microphone. Instead, he generally stayed fairly still, occasionally opening his arms to the audience and dropping them back to his sides.

When Danny Wilson enters the stage before performing "All of Me," it is quickly apparent that we are seeing a very different version of a 1940s Frank

---

[23] Keightley, "Frank Sinatra, Hi-Fi, and Formations of Adult Culture," 138.

Figure 5.1 Danny Wilson (Frank Sinatra) performs "All of Me" in *Meet Danny Wilson* (Universal Pictures, 1952).

Sinatra. For while the screaming fans represented his primary 1940s audience, the physical and confident way in which Danny Wilson carries himself is a stark contrast from the more restrained performance mannerisms of early Sinatra. Danny Wilson walks briskly on stage while waving, and even bends down into the audience to taste a cake bearing the frosted words "We Love Danny." He then proceeds to aggressively clap in time as the song begins, pausing to "shush" the audience with his hands so that he may begin. Throughout his performance, Wilson continuously moves from side to side, swings his arms, and confidently blows kisses as the girls in the audience sigh and yell words of adoration to the stage (Figure 5.1). In terms of musical style, Danny Wilson swings his rhythms harder and drops the ends of phrases more forcefully than Sinatra did throughout the 1940s. Wilson also alternates between more lyrical singing and a kind of declamatory style. Although Sinatra's musical performances in *Meet Danny Wilson* exhibit confidence, an analysis of the music's structural positions in the film using segmentation serves to reveal how Sinatra as Danny Wilson reflected the anxieties and struggles of some postwar Americans.

Raymond Bellour explains how classical Hollywood cinema relies on "rhyming" effects, noting that "the classical film from beginning to end is constantly repeating itself because it is resolving itself."[24] *Meet Danny Wilson* exemplifies the technique of rhyming most notably using certain musical numbers in a way that reveals the trajectory of Wilson's life. The film can be divided into forty segments (not including the opening credits), with Wilson's performance of "All of Me" as the very center in segment 20 (Table 5.1). The performance of "All of Me" represents the height of Wilson's career and personal life, with an ascent and descent on either side. It is in the

---

[24] Raymond Bellour, "Segmenting/Analyzing," in *Genre: The Musical*, ed. Rick Altman (London: Routledge and Kegan Paul and the British Film Institute, 1981), 66.

Segment	Song	Scenario
1		Opening scene
2	"You're a Sweetheart"	Drunk man heckles Danny's performance.
11	"A Good Man is Hard to Find"	Performed by Joy. Danny's first night working in Driscoll's club.
20	"All of Me"/"When You're Smiling"	High point of Danny's stardom and personal life.
28	"A Good Man is Hard to Find"	Duet between Danny and Joy. Obviously strained relationship.
33	"You're a Sweetheart"	Drunk Danny heckles audience.
34	"When You're Smiling"	Low point of Danny's narrative. Hears himself on jukebox while sitting in bar.
40		Final scene

Figure 5.2 Segmentation of musical numbers in *Meet Danny Wilson* (Universal Pictures, 1952).

segments surrounding the center point of "All of Me" that we see rhyming musical performances. Toward the very beginning of the film in segment 2, we see and hear Wilson's first musical performance, "You're a Sweetheart." This performance takes place in a loud, run-down bar, as Wilson and Ryan are still struggling to find steady work. The performance is constantly disrupted by oblivious customers and by a singularly inebriated man who heckles Wilson, provoking him to fight. This scene is mirrored toward the end of the film in segment 33, after Wilson has discovered that Carroll is in fact in love with Ryan, and his life begins spiraling out of control. Segment 33 is set in a much more upscale nightclub than in segment 2, after Wilson has already achieved international fame. Though he has found financial success, Wilson's personal life is in shambles, and he becomes the drunk heckler from segment 2, offending Ryan in public and proceeding to attempt an inebriated performance of "You're a Sweetheart," which ends in embarrassment and a severed friendship with Ryan.

A similar rhyming effect happens between segments 11 and 28, in which Wilson and Carroll perform "A Good Man Is Hard to Find." Carroll first performs this song in segment 11 in Nick Driscoll's nightclub, on Wilson's first night of successful employment, before she has formed any romantic attachment to either Wilson or Ryan. In segment 28, Wilson and Carroll perform the song together after it has become apparent to the viewer that Wilson has lost control of his personal life and Carroll is in love with Ryan, resulting in an uncomfortable duet in which Wilson tries to force and solidify Carroll's false love for him. Also in segment 11 is Wilson's first performance of "When You're Smiling," which we hear not once but twice more in the film. The second time we hear "When You're Smiling" is in the center segment, 20, alongside "All of Me." The first two instances of "When You're Smiling" work to establish it as Wilson's most recognizable hit. In segment 34, we do not see Wilson perform the song live, but instead find him in an almost empty bar trying to cope with the loss of both Ryan and Carroll. As he drinks, another customer turns on the jukebox, which plays Wilson's own recording of "When You're Smiling," sending Wilson into further despair.

All of these musical examples of rhyming work to show the dark reality of Danny Wilson's success, which in turn reflects the reality of America's "success" in World War II. Siegfried Kracauer makes reference to this idea of portraying deceptively positive events in film, such as those in the first half of *Meet Danny Wilson*, noting, "the more incorrectly they [contemporary films] present the surface of things, the more correct they become and the more clearly they mirror the secret mechanism of society."[25] In the case of *Meet Danny Wilson*, the surface appearance of Wilson's success in the first half of the film not only transitions into the harsh reality of Wilson's personal life, but reflects a similar reality of postwar America. This is most evident in *Meet Danny Wilson* when we learn that both Danny Wilson and Mike Ryan are veterans of World War II and are not afraid to vocalize their negative feelings toward their wartime experiences. In fact, Wilson and Ryan did not voluntarily enlist for the war. Instead, we find out through a dialogue between Carroll and Wilson that the FBI had to track down the two men to force them into service. After Carroll asks Wilson if they enlisted, he responds, "Enlist? What are you clownin'? Took the FBI three months to smoke us outta the gaiety. We were dancing in the line as girls." This revelation highlights further the isolation Danny Wilson feels from mainstream World War II expectations of American masculinity and patriotism, in that he not only tried to avoid service, but did so by disguising himself as a woman.

Portraying a character who admitted to avoiding service in *Meet Danny Wilson* was also a risk for Sinatra himself, who had already suffered scrutiny over his lack of active duty during World War II. But although this may have raised some eyebrows, the character of Danny Wilson in fact reflected fairly accurate postwar feelings that many American men who served in the war would have sympathized with. Mike Chopra-Gant explains how during the war, participation in the military gave many American men a strong sense

---

[25] Siegfried Kracauer, *The Mass Ornament*, trans. Thomas Y. Levin (Cambridge, MA: Harvard University Press, 1995), 292.

of identity, enhanced by uniforms, routine, and a directional sense of purpose.[26] But after the war ended, many American men experienced a crisis of identity, especially in terms of gender roles, that lacked the patriotism and sense of direction felt during the war, leaving veterans to remember only the negative aspects of their wartime experiences. These feelings were made worse by the newly realized and constant fear of nuclear warfare and tensions that accompanied the start of the Cold War. Because of this drastically different political and cultural climate, playing a character who was clearly isolated from and negative about his experience in World War II was not only less risky for Sinatra's career than it would have been in the years of World War II, but explicitly relatable to postwar men.

Despite, or also because of, Sinatra's real and raw portrayal of a jaded American man in both *Meet Danny Wilson* and *From Here to Eternity*, he faced public accusations of communist leanings in the 1950s, which in turn once again raised questions about his masculinity. K. A. Cuordileone notes how Cold War ideas of American femininity and masculinity were strongly linked with political affiliations. Citing the work of sociologist Daniel Bell, Cuordileone describes how national fears of both local and global communism sparked witch hunts toward those who leaned to the political left, which was viewed as more feminine and "soft" than the political right.[27] Non-mainstream-conforming characteristics, particularly in terms of gender and sexuality, increasingly became equated with communism as the nation's sense of identity and security continued to rely on conformity. Wini Breines explains, for example, how "Popular imagery and rhetoric coupled delinquency, homosexuality, and domineering mothers with communism, seeing them as joint dangers to the home and family, the heart of the American way of life."[28] Cuordileone summarizes this singular set of national ideas, indicating how they reflected a "political culture that put a new premium on hard masculine toughness and rendered anything less than that soft and feminine and, as such, a real or potential threat to the security of the nation."[29]

It is not surprising that Sinatra fell victim to the communist witch hunts of the 1950s when one considers the combination of his ambiguously white

---

[26] Mike Chopra-Gant, *Hollywood Genres and Postwar America: Masculinity, Family and Nation in Popular Movies and Film Noir* (London: I. B. Tauris, 2006).

[27] K. A. Cuordileone, "'Politics in an Age of Anxiety': Cold War Political Culture and the Crisis in American Masculinity, 1949–1960," *Journal of American History* 87, no. 2 (September 2000): 516.

[28] Breines, *Young, White, and Miserable*, 9.

[29] Cuordileone, "'Politics in an Age of Anxiety,'" 516.

Italian American background, his displays of different kinds of vulnerability beginning in World War II, his public affairs and rejection of traditional family life, and his political leanings. What is perhaps surprising is how, despite these accusations and personal experiences, Sinatra was still able to transform himself into one of the most popular American icons for decades to come. As Keightley suggests, this shift happened in 1952 in *From Here to Eternity*, while Karen McNally credits this transformation to Sinatra's 1954 film *Young at Heart*, in which McNally writes that

> Sinatra's performance commences a shift away from the feminizing vulnerability of his 1940s persona to an emotional expressiveness conveyed from a more masculine perspective. The role additionally defines the bitter and alienated working-class persona that underpins Sinatra's screen image through the 1950s, as both character and star are closely associated with career failure, highlighting their exclusion from the post-war American success story.[30]

While McNally accurately portrays Sinatra's role in *Young at Heart*, we can find cinematic evidence of this newly constructed image in *Meet Danny Wilson*, two years before *Young at Heart* and one year before *From Here to Eternity*. Although *Meet Danny Wilson* was quickly overshadowed by Sinatra's Oscar-winning performance the following year, it nevertheless serves as a window into the less visible and optimistic side of postwar American culture.

Conclusion

While the immediate postwar years were simultaneously defined by images of economic prosperity and domestic bliss coupled with extreme societal changes and feelings of anxiety and uncertainty for many Americans, we can end this study of Frank Sinatra and his war-era female fans rather cleanly with an article written by gossip columnist Hedda Hopper in 1949. The *Los Angeles Times* article, titled "Sinatra and Fans Grow Up in Tune: 'The Voice'

---

[30] Karen McNally, "'Where's the Spinning Wheel?': Frank Sinatra and Working-Class Alienation in *Young at Heart*," *Journal of American Studies* 41, no. 1 (April 2007): 127.

Has Mellowed Like His Bobby Soxers," suggests an obvious end to the era of Sinatra's bobbysoxers, though this end is not necessarily negative. Rather, Hopper writes with a feeling of calm acceptance about the impending shift in Sinatra's career, as well as the new lives his former teen fans will begin to pursue. Excerpts of the article are worth quoting in length:

> Frank's changed a lot since he first hit this town. First, it was the story about the bobby soxers who swarmed over him. Then he got in wrong with the press and got his brains beat out. One story led to another. Seemed he could satisfy no one.
>
> Then he had a little unhappiness with his wife Nancy. That got his fans down on him. People were saying he was a flash in the pan; he'd never last, nor would his voice....
>
> I remember a scene during the war—the first time he ever appeared on a Command Performance broadcast for our fellows overseas with Bing Crosby....
>
> I asked Bing about it later, and he said, "Listen, any guy that's made as many friends and fans as Frankie has in such a short time has got something. We need fellows like him; don't sell him short; encourage him. He's okay. He's going to do okay, too."
>
> Frank's proving every day the soundness of Bing's opinion....
>
> I asked whether the bobby soxers who originally swept him to success still were loyal to his cause. Frankie said, "Those kids have never let me forget they're my friends. But you can't call them bobby soxers any more. They've used the eight years since they first got behind me to good advantage."...
>
> Frank Sinatra's also grabbing a better way of life. He's got his feet on the ground and his eyes on the future. Like his bobby soxers, Frankie has grown up.[31]

This article seems to perfectly capture the state of Sinatra and his fans at the end of the 1940s. Sinatra endured a string of personal and career failures. Some of his former fans condemned him for it, but many others did not. However, although Sinatra would soon prove capable of building an even bigger fan base than before—comprising both men and women—which

---

[31] Hedda Hopper, "Sinatra and Fans Grow Up in Tune: 'The Voice' Has Mellowed Like His Bobby Soxers," *Los Angeles Times*, May 1, 1949, D1.

would last for decades, the fact was that Sinatra's postwar celebrity identity coupled with the drastic changes and pressures American women and girls encountered meant that Sinatra was no longer what the war-era bobbysoxers needed. And in turn, they were no longer what he needed. Rather than Sinatra and his fans having simply "grown up" as Hopper suggests, however—because as this book has demonstrated, war-era teenage fans in fact demonstrated a great deal of maturity during the war—it is more accurate to describe them both as having adapted: adapted to postwar expectations, anxieties, and their own sense of identity. And while the bobbysoxers of the 1940s mark a relatively short stop in the grand scheme of both Sinatra's lengthy career and twentieth-century American history, we can see how their experiences, values, and significantly their fandom reveal new and clear insight into World War II and postwar American culture.

Conclusion

Popular Remembrance

The year 2015 marked what would have been Frank Sinatra's 100th birthday. As Sinatra was—and still is—strongly established as an American icon, the year saw a variety of large-scale celebrations of the singer's career and legacy. A traveling museum exhibit, for example, titled *Sinatra: An American Icon* allowed visitors of the New York Library for the Performing Arts, the GRAMMY Museum, and the HistoryMiami Museum a glimpse into some of the artifacts that marked Sinatra's nearly sixty-year career. GRAMMY also produced a massive televised celebration concert in December 2015 celebrating Sinatra, advertised as "Sinatra 100—An All-Star GRAMMY Concert," featuring performances by popular music artists such as Tony Bennett, Harry Connick Jr., Celine Dion, Quincy Jones, and Lady Gaga, among others. It was clear in 2015 that despite Sinatra's passing seventeen years prior in 1998, Sinatra was very much still a part of America's cultural identity.

But what aspects of Sinatra did these celebrations remember? Perhaps unsurprisingly, they largely focused on Sinatra's recording, film, live performance, and entrepreneurial career from about the mid-1950s on. Images of Sinatra in his signature fedora performing and living the high life with his Rat Pack crew permeated these media celebrations, with emphasis on Sinatra's mid-to-late-career hits such as "Luck Be a Lady," "Come Fly with Me," "New York, New York," and "My Way." Emphasis was also placed on Sinatra's business side as founder of Reprise Records in 1960, which earned him the nickname the "Chairman of the Board." All these celebrations and media representations indicated that popular collective memory most strongly remembers the sides of Sinatra that defined him as a "serious" and masculine artist—that is, his film and musical career beginning in the postwar period, his business acumen, and his association with other masculine popular culture icons.

Similarly, the years 2019 and 2020 brought worldwide attention to the seventy-fifth anniversary of the end of World War II. Again, it is interesting to examine what these events chose to highlight and remember about the war. In the United States, Great Britain, and France, many events focused on the 2019 anniversary of D-Day, when Allied troops landed on the beaches of Normandy, igniting a pivotal turning point in the war's direction. Institutions such as The National WWII Museum featured educational exhibits and events about the D-Day invasions. D-Day re-enactments and newspaper coverage were widespread and many ceremonial events attended by world leaders honored those soldiers who contributed to the ultimate Allied victory.

Tributes to American women who served and worked during the war also appeared in 2019 and 2020, with "Rosie the Riveter" still reigning in popular memory as the ultimate symbol of women's contributions to World War II. Local newspapers featured interviews with women who worked in war factories or joined the military, and images of Rosie the Riveter, especially the 1942 version by artist J. Howard Miller, continue to appear in popular culture.[1]

While all of these historical remembrances of both Frank Sinatra and World War II demonstrate the extreme impact both had on American culture, they neglected certain people and themes. In the 100th birthday celebrations of Frank Sinatra, his career in the 1940s was mentioned, but often as a sort of preface to what would become his "real" career beginning in the 1950s. The *Sinatra: An American Icon* exhibit, for example, stated in reference to Sinatra's acting career prior to 1953, "[Sinatra's] early films were fun and fluffy, but gradually he learned the art of acting and in 1953, he was cast as Private Angelo Maggio in *From Here to Eternity*."[2] The "Sinatra 100—An All-Star GRAMMY Concert" was advertised as celebrating the "Chairman of the Board," emphasizing Sinatra's persona beginning around 1960 on, and included few performances of Sinatra's hits from the 1940s, instead focusing on the songs and image Sinatra came to embody in later decades. And in celebrations and tributes surrounding the seventy-fifth anniversary of the end of World War II, media attention was devoted almost entirely to the contributions of adult men and women, and especially those who actively served in the military or worked in war factories. American youth were notably absent from these remembrances.

While largely overlooked in mass media, Sinatra's early career has not been entirely forgotten. One revealing tribute to Sinatra after his death in

---

[1] See Figure 1.1 in Chapter 1.
[2] *Sinatra: An American Icon*, New York Public Library for the Performing Arts, New York, NY (2015).

the Summer–Fall 1999 issue of the Sidnatra Club's[3] newsletter, *The Sidnatra Club Update*, reveals that at least fifty years after World War II, Sinatra's older audience still remembered his wartime persona and performances. An excerpt from the tribute, which was initially published in *Car Collector* magazine and titled "A Part We Can't Replace: A Time We Won't Forget," reads:

> those of us in the World War II generation who were around from Frank's beginning probably felt we knew more about him, his songs and his life than most of today's news researchers and writers who were pulling together the highlights of his career and editing the tapes for TV.... Whatever, they missed a part of his life by which a lot of us in the World War II generation remember and love him best. For us it wasn't all the later stuff, food as it was, that younger people might relate to, snap their fingers to, like New York New York, and it sure wasn't the man with the crinkly voice on his last album with Willie and Steve and Edie and Tony and Barbara. That didn't say anything about what it was like to grow up and go through a war and the first 30 years with him.[4]

This tribute to Sinatra's wartime career was notably written by a man, as were all of the other articles published in this issue of the newsletter. As has been noted throughout this study, active Sinatra fandom during the years of the war was largely female, though instances of male fan club members do appear periodically in club journals.[5] In an era when male strength—both physical and emotional—defined American ideals of masculinity, men were not encouraged to express feelings of vulnerability, sentimentality, or fear. This tribute reveals, however, that many American men did experience these emotions during the war and may have turned to Sinatra in a more private way than female fans did. The tribute suggests an acute awareness of this, continuing:

> The girls talked about his soft voice, and his vulnerable, little boy looks, but the boys didn't say anything. We simply used him, realizing that our emotionally tongue-tied generation had needed him or someone like him from

---

[3] The club's name is a combination of Sinatra's and Philadelphia radio disc jockey Sid Mark's. Mark is noted for hosting radio programming dedicated to Sinatra.

[4] Thomas D. Murray, "A Part We Can't Replace: A Time We Won't Forget," *Car Collector* (September 1998), quoted in *The Sidnatra Club Update* (Summer–Fall 1999), 3, author's personal collection.

[5] See Chapter 4.

the minute we discovered the opposite sex. All the things we couldn't say he not only said for us, but he sang them for us, convincingly, disarmingly, dramatically.[6]

This revealing insight into male experiences with Sinatra during World War II—which some men may not have felt comfortable admitting to until years later—would prove fruitful for future study of war-era Sinatra fandom and American identity. But as this tribute indicates, this book has focused on Sinatra's female wartime fans, because they were the ones who "talked about his soft voice, and his vulnerable, little boy looks." They were the ones who wrote, published, and publicly vocalized their opinions on Sinatra. Thus, this book has used the materials and practices of World War II–era Frank Sinatra fan clubs—the membership of which was overwhelmingly teenaged and female—to challenge historical remembrance of war-era American teenage girls as distracted and obsessed with a popular idol amid national crisis. The materials and texts created by these fans instead shed light on productive communities of young citizens who desired to foster connections with one another and the entertainment industry, contribute to the war effort, discuss important topics such as racial and religious tolerance, develop professional skills, and above all, safely and creatively express their admiration of Sinatra and their opinions on popular culture among understanding peers.

While the fan-made objects featured in this study have some limits and do not necessarily represent the experiences of all wartime teenage girls or fans of popular music, they nevertheless work to paint an exceptionally clear picture about how one specific fan community used their popular music fandom simultaneously as a springboard for pursuing roles as active citizens when society did not provide them with a clear purpose, and as safe and open spaces to express their personal desires while being influenced by contradictory external messages regarding gender and sexual expectations. Adding a new story to America's narratives of World War II and popular culture by examining sources created not by commercial media, but by independent participants and fans from these cultures, we find in the short-lived yet singular relationship between Frank Sinatra and World War II American teenage girls new layers in the complex fabric of wartime gender roles, values, and the interconnectivity of popular culture and society.

---

[6] Murray, "A Part We Can't Replace," 3.

Bibliography

Altman, Rick. *The American Film Musical*. Bloomington: Indiana University Press, 1987.
Anderson, Benedict. *Imagined Communities: Reflections on the Origin and Spread of Nationalism*. London: Verso, 2006.
Anderson, Karen. *Wartime Women: Sex Roles, Family Relations, and the Status of Women During World War II*. Westport, CT: Greenwood, 1981.
Anselmo, Diana W. *A Queer Way of Feeling: Girl Fans and Personal Archives of Early Hollywood*. Oakland: University of California Press, 2023.
Associated Youth-Serving Organizations, Inc. *On Teen-Age Canteens: A Memorandum*. October 1944. Oregon State Archives. sos.oregon.gov/archives.
Baade, Christina. *Victory through Harmony: The BBC and Popular Music in World War II*. New York: Oxford University Press, 2012.
Barbas, Samantha. *Movie Crazy: Fans, Stars, and the Cult of Celebrity*. New York: Palgrave, 2001.
Bederman, Gail. *Manliness & Civilization: A Cultural History of Gender and Race in the United States, 1880–1917*. Chicago: University of Chicago Press, 1995.
Beisel Hollenbach, Katie. "'I Hear Music When I Look at You': Teenage Agency, Mass Media, and Frank Sinatra in World War II America." PhD diss., University of Illinois, 2018.
Beisel Hollenbach, Katie. "Teenage Agency and Popular Music Reception in World War II-Era Frank Sinatra Fan Clubs." *Journal of Popular Music Studies* 31, no. 4 (Winter 2019): 142–160.
Bellour, Raymond. "Segmenting/Analyzing." In *Genre: The Musical*, edited by Rick Altman, 66–92. London: Routledge and Kegan Paul and the British Film Institute, 1981.
Bernstein, Robin. *Racial Innocence: Performing Childhood and Race from Slavery to Civil Rights*. New York: New York University Press, 2011.
Bérubé, Allan. *Coming Out under Fire: The History of Gay Men and Women in World War Two*. New York: Free Press, 1990.
Bolling, Ben, and Matthew J. Smith, eds. *It Happens at Comic-Con: Ethnographic Essays on a Pop Culture Phenomenon*. Jefferson, NC: McFarland & Co., 2014.
Booker, Janice L. "Why the Bobby Soxers?" In *Frank Sinatra: History, Identity, and Italian American Culture*, edited by Stanislao G. Pugliese, 73–82. New York: Palgrave Macmillan, 2004.
Breines, Wini. "The 'Other' Fifties: Beats and Bad Girls." In *Not June Cleaver: Women and Gender in Postwar America, 1945–1960*, edited by Joanne Meyerowitz, 382–408. Philadelphia: Temple University Press, 1994.
Breines, Wini. *Young, White, and Miserable: Growing Up Female in the Fifties*. Boston: Beacon Press, 1992.
Brickman, Barbara Jane. "This Charming Butch: The Male Pop Idol, Girl Fans, and Lesbian (in)Visibility." *Journal of Popular Music Studies* 28, no. 4 (2016): 443–459.
Brownell, Kathryn Cramer. *Showbiz Politics: Hollywood in American Political Life*. Chapel Hill: University of North Carolina Press, 2014.
Butler, Judith. *Undoing Gender*. New York: Routledge, 2004.
Campbell, D'Ann. *Women at War with America: Private Lives in a Patriotic Era*. Cambridge, MA: Harvard University Press, 1984.
Caputo, Virginia, and Karen Pegley. "Growing Up Female(s): Retrospective Thoughts on Musical Preferences and Meanings." In *Queering the Pitch: The New Gay and Lesbian Musicology*, edited by Philip Brett, Elizabeth Wood, and Gary C. Thomas, 297–314. New York: Routledge, 1994.

Cavicchi, Daniel. *Listening and Longing: Music Lovers in the Age of Barnum.* Middletown, CT: Wesleyan University Press, 2011.

Chauncey, George. *Gay New York: Gender, Urban Culture, and the Making of the Gay Male World, 1890–1940.* New York: Basic Books, 1994.

Chopra-Gant, Mike. *Hollywood Genres and Postwar America: Masculinity, Family and Nation in Popular Movies and Film Noir.* London: I. B. Tauris. 2006.

Citron, Marcia J. *Gender and the Musical Canon.* Cambridge: Cambridge University Press, 1993.

Click, Melissa A., and Suzanne Scott. "Introduction." In *The Routledge Companion to Media Fandom,* edited by Melissa A. Click and Suzanne Scott, 1–5. New York: Routledge, 2018.

Coates, Norma. "Teenyboppers, Groupies, and Other Grotesques: Girls and Women in Rock Culture in the 1960s and early 1970s." *Journal of Popular Music Studies* 15, no. 1 (2003): 65–94.

Cooper, B. Lee. "From 'Love Letters' to 'Miss You': Popular Recordings, Epistolary Imagery, and Romance during War-Time, 1941–1945." *Journal of American Culture* 19, no. 4 (1996): 15–27.

Coppa, Francesca. "Fuck Yeah, Fandom Is Beautiful." *Journal of Fandom Studies* 2, no. 1 (2014): 73–82.

Cuordileone, K. A. "'Politics in an Age of Anxiety': Cold War Political Culture and the Crisis in American Masculinity, 1949–1960." *Journal of American History* 87, no. 2 (September 2000): 515–545.

de Lauretis, Teresa. *The Practice of Love: Lesbian Sexuality and Perverse Desire.* Bloomington: Indiana University Press, 1994).

Dingle, Christopher. "Introduction." In *The Cambridge History of Music Criticism,* edited by Christopher Dingle, 1–5. Cambridge: Cambridge University Press, 2019.

Doss, Erika. *Elvis Culture: Fans, Faith & Image.* Lawrence: University Press of Kansas, 1999.

Douglas, Susan J. *Listening In: Radio and the American Imagination.* Minneapolis: University of Minnesota Press, 2004.

Duffett, Mark. *Understanding Fandom: An Introduction to the Study of Media Fan Culture.* New York: Bloomsbury Academic, 2013.

Dunn, Kevin, and May Summer Farnsworth. "'We ARE the Revolution': Riot Grrrl Press, Girl Empowerment, and DIY Self-Publishing." *Women's Studies* 41, no. 2 (2012): 136–157.

Dyer, Richard. *Heavenly Bodies: Film Stars and Society.* New York: St. Martin's Press, 1986.

Dyer, Richard. *Stars.* London: British Film Institute, 1998.

Dyer, Richard. *White.* London: Routledge, 1997.

Ehrenreich, Barbara, Elizabeth Hess, and Gloria Jacobs. "Beatlemania: Girls Just Want to Have Fun." In *The Adoring Audience: Fan Culture and Popular Media,* edited by Lisa A. Lewis, 84–106. London: Routledge, 1992.

Erenberg, Lewis A. *Swingin' the Dream: Big Band Jazz and the Rebirth of American Culture.* Chicago: University of Chicago Press, 1998.

Erenberg, Lewis A., and Susan E. Hirsch, eds. *The War in American Culture: Society and Consciousness during World War II.* Chicago: University of Chicago Press, 1996.

Farmer, Brett. "Queer Negotiations of the Hollywood Cinema." In *Queer Cinema: The Film Reader,* edited by Harry M. Benshoff and Sean Griffin, 75–88. New York: Routledge, 2004.

Fleming, William L. "The Venereal Disease Problem in the United States in World War II." *Journal of the Elisha Mitchell Scientific Society* 61, no. 1/2 (August 1945): 195–200.

Foster, Gwendolyn Audrey. *Performing Whiteness.* Albany: State University of New York Press, 2003.

Fousek, John. *To Lead the Free World: American Nationalism & the Cultural Roots of the Cold War.* Chapel Hill: University of North Carolina Press, 2000.

Frankenberg, Ruth. *White Women, Race Matters: The Social Construction of Whiteness.* Minneapolis: University of Minnesota Press. 1993.

Friedwald, Will. *Sinatra! The Song Is You: A Singer's Art.* New York: Scribner, 1995.

Frith, Simon, and Angela McRobbie. "Rock and Sexuality." In *On Record: Rock, Pop and the Written Word*, edited by Simon Frith and Andrew Goodwin, 371–389. London: Routledge, 1990.

Fuller, Kathryn H. *At the Picture Show: Small-Town Audiences and the Creation of Movie Fan Culture*. Washington, DC: Smithsonian Institution Press, 1996.

Fuller-Seeley, Kathryn H. "Archaeologies of Fandom: Using Historical Methods to Explore Fan Cultures of the Past." In *The Routledge Companion to Media Fandom*, edited by Melissa A. Click and Suzanne Scott, 27–35. New York: Routledge, 2018.

Fuller-Seeley, Kathryn H. "Dish Night at the Movies: Exhibitor Promotions and Female Audiences during the Great Depression." In *Looking Past the Screen: Case Studies in American Film History and Method*, edited by Jon Lewis and Eric Smoodin, 246–275. Durham, NC: Duke University Press, 2007.

Gaines, Jane. "War, Women, and Lipstick: Fan Mags in the Forties." *Heresies* 5, no. 18 (1985): 42–47.

Gavin, Lettie. *American Women in World War I: They Also Served*. Niwot: University Press of Colorado, 1997.

Gennari, John. "Passing for Italian: Crooners and Gangsters in Crossover Culture." In *Frank Sinatra: History, Identity, and Italian American Culture*, edited by Stanislao G. Pugliese, 147–154. New York: Palgrave Macmillan, 2004.

Genné, Beth. "'Freedom Incarnate': Jerome Robbins, Gene Kelly, and the Dancing Sailor as an Icon of American Values in World War II." *Dance Chronicle* 24, no. 1 (2001): 83–103.

Giddins, Gary. *Bing Crosby: A Pocketful of Dreams. The Early Years, 1903–1940*. Boston: Little, Brown, 2001.

Gilbert, Roger. "Beloved and Notorious: A Theory of American Stardom, with Special Reference to Bing Crosby and Frank Sinatra." *Southwest Review* 95, no. 1/2 (2010): 167–184.

Giordano, Ralph G. *Social Dancing in America: A History and Reference*, Vol. 2: *Lindy Hop to Hip Hop, 1901–2000*. Westport, CT: Greenwood, 2007.

Glickman, Lawrence B., ed. *Consumer Society in American History: A Reader*. Ithaca, NY: Cornell University Press, 1999.

Goldmark, Daniel. *Tunes for 'Toons: Music and the Hollywood Cartoon*. Berkeley: University of California Press, 2005.

Gordon, Dorothy. "As the Youngsters See Juvenile Delinquency: They Think Grown-Ups Misjudge the Causes and Propose Some Measures of Their Own." *New York Times*, August 6, 1944, 16.

Gottlieb, Joanne, and Gayle Wald. "Smells Like Teen Spirit: Riot Grrrls, Revolution and Women in Independent Rock." In *Microphone Fiends: Youth Music & Youth Culture*, edited by Andrew Ross and Tricia Rose, 250–274. New York: Routledge, 1994.

Granata, Charles L. *Sessions with Sinatra: Frank Sinatra and the Art of Recording*. Chicago: A Cappella Books, 2004.

Gray, Jonathan, Cornel Sandvoss, and C. Lee Harrington. "Introduction: Why Still Study Fans?" In *Second Edition: Identities and Communities in a Mediated World*, edited by Jonathan Gray, Cornel Sandvoss, and C. Lee Harrington, 1–26. New York: New York University Press, 2017.

Grossberg, Lawrence. "Is There a Fan in the House?: The Affective Sensibility of Fandom." In *The Adoring Audience: Fan Culture and Popular Media*, edited by Lisa A. Lewis, 50–65. London: Routledge, 1992.

Guerra, Paula, and Pedro Quintela, eds. *Punk, Fanzines and DIY Cultures in a Global World: Fast, Furious and Xerox*. Cham, Switzerland: Palgrave Macmillan, 2020.

Hall, Martha L., Belinda T. Orzada, and Dilia Lopez-Gydosh. "American Women's Wartime Dress: Sociocultural Ambiguity Regarding Women's Roles during World War II." *Journal of American Culture* 38, no. 3 (September 2015): 232–242.

Hamer, Laura. "The Gender Paradox: Criticism of Women and Women as Critics." In *The Cambridge History of Music Criticism*, edited by Christopher Dingle, 272–290. Cambridge: Cambridge University Press, 2019.

Hamill, Pete. *Why Sinatra Matters*. Boston: Little, Brown, 1998.

Hansen, Miriam. *Babel and Babylon: Spectatorship in American Silent* Film. Cambridge, MA: Harvard University Press, 1991.
Hegarty, Marilyn E. *Victory Girls, Khaki-Wackies, and Patriotutes: The Regulation of Female Sexuality during World War II*. New York: New York University Press, 2008.
Hilmes, Michele. *Hollywood and Broadcasting: From Radio to Cable*. Urbana: University of Illinois Press, 1990.
Hilmes, Michele. *Radio Voices: American Broadcasting, 1922–1952*. Minneapolis: University of Minnesota Press, 1997.
Hinerman, Stephen. "'I'll Be Here with You': Fans, Fantasy and the Figure of Elvis." In *The Adoring Audience: Fan Culture and Popular Media*, edited by Lisa A. Lewis, 107–134. London: Routledge, 1992.
Holub, Robert C. *Reception Theory: A Critical Introduction*. London: Methuen, 1984.
Honey, Maureen. *Bitter Fruit: African American Women in World War II*. Columbia: University of Missouri Press, 1999.
Horten, Gerd. *Radio Goes to War: The Cultural Politics of Propaganda during World War II*. Berkeley: University of California Press, 2002.
Jacklosky, Rob. "'Someone to Watch over Him': Images of Class and Gender Vulnerability in Early Sinatra." In *Frank Sinatra: History, Identity, and Italian American Culture*, edited by Stanislao G. Pugliese, 91–100. New York: Palgrave Macmillan, 2004.
Jacobson, Matthew Frye. *Whiteness of a Different Color: European Immigrants and the Alchemy of Race*. Cambridge, MA: Harvard University Press, 1999.
Jarman-Ivens, Freya, ed. *Oh Boy!: Masculinities and Popular Music*. New York: Routledge, 2007.
Jarvis, Christina S. *The Male Body at War: American Masculinity during World War II*. DeKalb: Northern Illinois University Press, 2010.
Jauss, Hans Robert. *Toward an Aesthetic of Reception*. Translated by Timothy Bahti. Minneapolis: University of Minnesota Press, 1982.
Jenkins, Henry. *Fans, Bloggers, and Gamers: Exploring Participatory Culture*. New York: New York University Press, 2006.
Jenkins, Henry. *Textual Poachers: Television Fans and Participatory Culture*. New York: Routledge, 2013.
Jenkins, Henry, and John Tulloch. *Science Fiction Audiences: Watching "Dr. Who" and "Star Trek"*. London: Routledge, 1995.
Jones, John Bush. *The Songs That Fought the War: Popular Music and the Home Front, 1939–1945*. Lebanon, NH: Brandeis University Press, 2006.
Juliani, Richard N. "Italian Americans and Their Religious Experience." In *The Routledge History of Italian Americans*, edited by William J. Connell and Stanislao G. Pugliese, 193–211. New York: Routledge, 2018.
Kahn, E. J., Jr. *The Voice: The Story of an American Phenomenon*. New York: Harper & Brothers, 1946.
Kaplan, James. *Frank: The Voice*. New York: Anchor Books, 2010.
Katz, Mark. *Capturing Sound: How Technology Has Changed Music*. Berkeley: University of California Press, 2010.
Kearney, Mary Celeste. "Producing Girls: Rethinking the Study of Female Youth Culture." In *Delinquents & Debutantes: Twentieth-Century American Girls' Cultures*, edited by Sherrie A. Inness, 285–310. New York: New York University Press, 1998.
Keightley, Keir. "Frank Sinatra, Hi-Fi, and Formations of Adult Culture: Gender, Technology, and Celebrity, 1948–62." PhD diss., Concordia University, 1996.
Kimmel, Michael. *Manhood in America: A Cultural History*. New York: Free Press, 1996.
Knaff, Donna B. *Beyond Rosie the Riveter: Women of World War II in American Popular Graphic Art*. Lawrence: University Press of Kansas, 2012.
Knapp, Raymond. *The American Musical and the Formation of National Identity*. Princeton, NJ: Princeton University Press, 2005.

Kompare, Derek. "Fan Curators and the Gateways into Fandom." In *The Routledge Companion to Media Fandom*, edited by Melissa A. Click and Suzanne Scott, 107–113. New York: Routledge, 2018.

Kracauer, Siegfried. *The Mass Ornament: Weimar Essays*. Translated by Thomas Y. Levin. Cambridge, MA: Harvard University Press, 1995.

Laing, Heather. *The Gendered Score: Music in 1940s Melodrama and the Women's Film*. Hampshire: Ashgate, 2007.

Leonard, Candy. *Beatleness: How the Beatles and Their Fans Remade the World*. New York: Arcade, 2014.

Leppert, Richard. *The Sight of Sound: Music, Representation, and the History of the Body*. Berkeley: University of California Press, 1993.

Lewis, Lisa A., ed. *The Adoring Audience: Fan Culture and Popular Media*. London: Routledge, 1992.

Lindberg, Ulf, Gestur Guðmundsson, Morten Michelsen, and Hans Weisethaunet. *Rock Criticism from the Beginning: Amusers, Bruisers, & Cool-Headed Cruisers*. New York: Peter Lang, 2005.

Lockheart, Paula. "A History of Early Microphone Singing, 1925–1939: American Mainstream Popular Singing at the Advent of Electronic Microphone Amplification." *Popular Music and Society* 26, no. 3 (2003): 367–385.

Luconi, Stefano. "Contested Loyalties: World War II and Italian-Americans' Ethnic Identity." *Italian Americana* 30, no. 2 (Summer 2012): 151–167.

McCloskey, Mark A. *Youth Centers: An Appraisal and a Look Ahead . . . Based on Nation-wide Survey*. Report for Federal Security Agency, Office of Community War Services, 1945. Washington, DC: Federal Security Agency.

McCracken, Allison. *Real Men Don't Sing: Crooning in American Culture*. Durham, NC: Duke University Press, 2015.

McDonald, Christopher J. *Rush, Rock Music, and the Middle Class: Dreaming in Middletown*. Bloomington: Indiana University Press, 2009.

McNally, Karen. "Sailors and Kissing Bandits: The Challenging Spectacle of Frank Sinatra at MGM." In *The Sound of Musicals*, edited by Steven Cohan, 93–103. London: British Film Institute, 2010.

McNally, Karen. *When Frankie Went to Hollywood: Frank Sinatra and American Male Identity*. Urbana: University of Illinois Press, 2008.

McNally, Karen. "'Where's the Spinning Wheel?': Frank Sinatra and Working-Class Alienation in *Young at Heart*." *Journal of American Studies* 41, no. 1 (April 2007): 115–133.

Meyerowitz, Joanne, ed. *Not June Cleaver: Women and Gender in Postwar America, 1945–1960*. Philadelphia: Temple University Press, 1994.

Millard, André. *Beatlemania: Technology, Business, and Teen Culture in Cold War America*. Baltimore: Johns Hopkins University Press, 2012.

Miller, Neil. *Out of the Past: Gay and Lesbian History from 1869 to the Present*. New York: Vintage Books, 1995.

Mills, Richard. *The Beatles and Fandom: Sex, Death and Progressive Nostalgia*. London: Bloomsbury Academic, 2019.

Morgan, Iwan, and Philip John Davies, eds. *Hollywood and the Great Depression: American Film, Politics and Society in the 1930s*. Edinburgh: Edinburgh University Press, 2016.

Morthland, John, ed. *Mainlines, Blood Feasts, and Bad Taste: A Lester Bangs Reader*. New York: Anchor Books, 2003.

Mullenbach, Cheryl. *Double Victory: How African American Women Broke Race and Gender Barriers to Help Win World War II*. Chicago: Chicago Review Press, 2013.

Mulvey, Laura. "Visual Pleasure and Narrative Cinema." In *Film Theory and Criticism: Introductory Readings*, edited by Leo Braudy and Marshall Cohen, 833–844. 5th ed. New York: Oxford University Press, 1999.

Murray, Matthew. "'The Tendency to Deprave and Corrupt Morals': Regulation and Irregular Sexuality in Golden Age Radio Comedy." In *Radio Reader: Essays in the Cultural History of Radio*, edited by Michele Hilmes and Jason Loviglio, 135–156. New York: Routledge, 2002.

Nott, James. *Music for the People: Popular Music and Dance in Interwar Britain*. Oxford: Oxford University Press, 2002.

Orgeron, Marsha. "'You Are Invited to Participate': Interactive Fandom in the Age of the Movie Magazine." *Journal of Film & Video* 61, no. 3 (Fall 2009): 3–23.

Palladino, Grace. *Teenagers: An American History*. New York: Basic Books, 1996.

Palter, Ruth. "Radio's Attraction for Housewives." *Hollywood Quarterly* 3, no. 3 (Spring 1948): 248–257.

Peiss, Kathy. *Hope in a Jar: The Making of America's Beauty Culture*. Philadelphia: University of Pennsylvania Press, 2011.

Petkov, Steven, and Leonard Mustazza, eds. *The Frank Sinatra Reader*. New York: Oxford University Press, 1995.

Polan, Dana. *Power and Paranoia: History, Narrative, and the American Cinema, 1940–1950*. New York: Columbia University Press, 1986.

Pretelli, Matteo. "Hollywood's Depiction of Italian American Servicemen during the Italian Campaign of World War II." *European Journal of American Studies* 15, no. 2 (Summer 2020): 1–18.

Pugliese, Stanislao G., ed. *Frank Sinatra: History, Identity, and Italian American Culture*. New York: Palgrave Macmillan, 2004.

Radway, Janice A. *Reading the Romance: Women, Patriarchy, and Popular Literature*. Chapel Hill: University of North Carolina Press, 1984.

Razlogova, Elena. *The Listener's Voice: Early Radio and the American Public*. Philadelphia: University of Pennsylvania Press, 2011.

Rhodes, Lisa L. *Electric Ladyland: Women and Rock Culture*. Philadelphia: University of Pennsylvania Press, 2005.

Roediger, David R. *Working toward Whiteness: How America's Immigrants Became White*. New York: Basic Books, 2005.

Samuel, Lawrence R. *Pledging Allegiance: American Identity and the Bond Drive of World War II*. Washington, DC: Smithsonian Institution Press, 1997.

Savage, Jon. *Teenage: The Prehistory of Youth Culture: 1875–1945*. London: Penguin, 2007.

Schrum, Kelly. *Some Wore Bobby Sox: The Emergence of Teenage Girls' Culture, 1920–1945*. New York: Palgrave Macmillan, 2004.

Schrum, Kelly. "'Teena Means Business': Teenage Girls' Culture and 'Seventeen' Magazine, 1944–1950." In *Delinquents & Debutantes: Twentieth-Century American Girls' Cultures*, edited by Sherrie A. Inness, 134–163. New York: New York University Press, 1998.

Scott, Suzanne. *Fake Geek Girls: Fandom, Gender, and the Convergence Culture Industry*. New York: New York University Press, 2019.

Slide, Anthony. *Inside the Hollywood Fan Magazine: A History of Star Makers, Fabricators, and Gossip Mongers*. Jackson: University Press of Mississippi, 2010.

Smith, Kathleen E. R. *God Bless America: Tin Pan Alley Goes to War*. Lexington: University Press of Kentucky, 2015.

Smith, Michelle. "In Rosie's Shadow: World War II Recruitment Rhetoric and Women's Work in Public Memory." In *Women at Work: Rhetorics of Gender and Labor*, edited by David Gold and Jessica Enoch, 186–208. Pittsburgh: University of Pittsburgh Press, 2019.

Stacey, Jackie. *Star Gazing: Hollywood Cinema and Female Spectatorship*. London: Routledge, 1994.

Stanfill, Mel. "The Unbearable Whiteness of Fandom and Fan Studies." In *A Companion to Media Fandom and Fan Studies*, edited by Paul Booth, 305–317. Hoboken, NJ: John Wiley & Sons, 2018.

Stowe, David W. *Swing Changes: Big Band Jazz in New Deal America*. Cambridge, MA: Harvard University Press, 1994.

Studlar, Galyn. "The Perils of Pleasure? Fan Magazine Discourse as Women's Commodified Culture in the 1920s." In *Silent Film*, edited by Richard Abel, 263–297. New Brunswick, NJ: Rutgers University Press, 1996.

Studlar, Gayln. *This Mad Masquerade: Stardom and Masculinity in the Jazz Age*. New York: Columbia University Press, 1996.

The Subcultures Network. *Ripped, Torn and Cut: Pop, Politics and Punk Fanzines from 1976*. Manchester: Manchester University Press, 2018.

Sweeney, Michael S. *Secrets of Victory: The Office of Censorship and the American Press and Radio in World War II*. Chapel Hill: University of North Carolina Press, 2001.

"Teen-Age Girls: They Live in a Wonderful World of their Own." *Life*, December 11, 1944, 91–99.

Thorp, Margaret Farrand. *America at the Movies*. New Haven, CT: Yale University Press, 1939.

Triggs, Teal. *Fanzines: The DIY Revolution*. San Francisco: Chronicle Books, 2010.

Trotter, Joe William, Jr. "From a Raw Deal to a New Deal? 1929–1945." In *To Make Our World Anew*, Vol. 3: *A History of African Americans since 1880*, edited by Robin D. G. Kelley and Earl Lewis, 131–166. New York: Oxford University Press, 2000.

Tucker, Sherrie. *Dance Floor Democracy: The Social Geography of Memory at the Hollywood Canteen*. Durham, NC: Duke University Press, 2014.

Tucker, Sherrie. *Swing Shift: "All-Girl" Bands of the 1940s*. Durham, NC: Duke University Press, 2001.

Vellon, Peter G. "Italian Americans and Race during the Era of Mass Immigration." In *The Routledge History of Italian Americans*, edited by William J. Connell and Stanislao G. Pugliese, 212–222. New York: Routledge, 2018.

Warsh, Cheryl Krasnick, and Dan Malleck, eds. *Consuming Modernity: Gendered Behaviour and Consumerism Before the Baby Boom*. Vancouver: University of British Columbia Press, 2013.

Weatherford, Doris. *American Women and World War II*. Edison, NJ: Castle Books, 2008.

Weatherford, Doris. *American Women during World War II: An Encyclopedia*. New York: Routledge, 2010.

Wertham, Fredric. *The World of Fanzines: A Special Form of Communication*. Carbondale: Southern Illinois University Press, 1973.

Yellin, Emily. *Our Mother's War: American Women at Home and at the Front during World War II*. New York: Free Press, 2004.

Archival Sources

Fan Magazines Collection. Media History Digital Library. http://mediahistoryproject.org.

Gertrude Soeurt collection of actor files, 1929–1960. Billy Rose Theatre Division. New York Public Library for the Performing Arts. New York, NY.

Hal Mohr and Evelyn Venable papers. Margaret Herrick Library. Academy of Motion Picture Arts and Sciences. Beverly Hills, CA.

Hedda Hopper papers. Margaret Herrick Library. Academy of Motion Picture Arts and Sciences. Beverly Hills, CA.

Paley Center Collections. Paley Center for Media. New York, NY.

Paul Henreid papers. Margaret Herrick Library. Academy of Motion Picture Arts and Sciences. Beverly Hills, CA.

Sinatra-ana Collection. Hoboken Historical Museum. Hoboken, NJ.

Stuart A. Rose Manuscript, Archives, and Rare Book Library. Emory University. Atlanta, GA.

Index

For the benefit of digital users, indexed terms that span two pages (e.g., 52–53) may, on occasion, appear on only one of those pages.

Note: Figures are indicated by an italic *f* following the page number.

Adopt a Foreign Fan Association (AAFFA), 12, 89–100
advice columns, 26–27, 30, 64
African Americans, 10, 18–20, 79–80, 88–89, 129–30
After Hours ads, 23–26, 25*f*
Aldrich, Betty, 107
All Star Bond Rally (1945), 32–34, 114
American Federation of Musicians, 3–4
Anderson, Harry, 93*f*
Associated Youth- Serving Organizations, Inc., 47, 50
Atlanta Constitution, 123–24
At the Picture Show: Small- Town Audiences and the Creation of Movie Fan Culture (Fuller), 63–64

Band Leaders magazine, 52, 57
Barbato, Nancy, 137–38
Beatles fandom, 5–6
Bellour, Raymond, 145–46
Bergquist, Esther, 111–12
Bergstrom, Frances, 52, 57
Billboard magazine, 31
Bolton Bill (1943), 17
Bond Rally Song, 33–34
Booker, Janice L., 81
BowTie Bugle, 55–56, 82, 85–86, 122, 124*f*
Breines, Wini, 136–37
Brickman, Barbara Jane, 120
Brundage, Lois, 117

Camay soap ads, 23–24, 24*f*
The Cambridge History of Music Criticism (Dingle), 101, 126–27
Campen, Gloria, 57, 58*f*
Capitol Records, 4
career slump, 4
Catholic Americans, 75–76
censorship, 54, 94

Chicago Daily Tribune, 37
Chicago Defender, 74, 131–32
Chopra- Gant, Mike, 147–48
Citron, Marcia J., 7–8, 12–13, 102–3
civil rights and politics
 fan writings on tolerance, 81–89, 84*f*
 foreign fan association, 89–100
 introduction to, 6, 12, 73–75, 136–37
 Italian American identity, 75–81
 nationalism, 89–100, 92*f*, 93*f*
Coates, Norma, 103
Cold War, 131, 133, 136, 140–41, 147–48
Columbus Day riot (1944), 43
communism, 37, 133, 148–49
Coppa, Francesca, 6–7
creative criticism in fan texts, 109–18
Crosby, Bing, 1, 3, 31–35, 38–39, 70, 76–77, 106–7, 113–15, 120, 130, 150
Cuordileone, K. A., 148

Daily Boston Globe, 91–92, 129, 132
death of Sinatra, 4
Delacorte, Al, 59–61
demographics of fan clubs, 55–58
digital fans, 6–7
Di Mattia, Irene, 94–95
Dingle, Christopher, 101, 109, 126–27
Diven, Marjorie, 12, 92–98
Dorsey, Tommy, 3, 144
Duffett, Mark, 54
Dunn, Kevin, 103
Dyer, Richard, 126

early life of Sinatra, 3–4
El Club Cabana magazine, 53
Ellovich, Elsie, 70–71
Erenberg, Lewis A., 32, 44
ethnicity/ethnic identity, 6, 9, 34–35, 76, 105, 134
Evans, George, 58–59

166 INDEX

Fair Labor Standards Act (1938), 10, 21–22
fan anonymity, 5–6, 9–10, 52–53, 57, 105–6
fan club journals, 52–55
Fan Club League, 53
fan demographics, 8–11, 55–58
fans as music and culture critics
    creative criticism in fan texts, 109–18
    gender and vulnerability, 118–26
    introduction to, 12–13, 101–4
    reader participation in fan magazines, 104–8
The Fans newsletter, 67
fan writings on tolerance, 81–89, 84*f*
fanzines, 54, 103, 104–5
Farnsworth, May Summer, 103
female sexuality, 22–23, 26–31, 39–40, 100, 120
feminization of Sinatra, 4
followers, 6–7, 8–9
foreign fan association, 89–100
Fousek, John, 133
Frankenberg, Ruth, 85
Frankie's United Swooners, 123–24
Frank Sinatra fan clubs
    entertainment industry and, 63–71
    gender and vulnerability in, 118–26
    journals, 52–55
    membership procedures and demographics, 55–58
    structures and business practices, 58–63
    thumbnail sketches, 55–56
Frank Sinatra Music Club, 83
Franz, Marilyn, 107
From Here to Eternity (1953), 4, 140–42, 143–44, 147–49, 154
Fuller, Kathryn H., 63–64

Gardner, Ava, 4, 141
Gender and the Musical Canon (Citron), 7–8
gender and vulnerability, 118–26
Gilbert, Roger, 34, 114–15
Goodman, Benny, 3–4
Grable, Betty, 2, 33, 106–7
Grayson, Kathryn, 107
Great Depression, 10, 21–22, 35–36, 63–64, 113, 133

Hamill, Pete, 79
Hammons, Bonnie, 123–25
Hansen, Miriam, 64–65
Hayworth, Rita, 2
Hegarty, Marilyn E., 11, 29
Heiskanen, Gloria, 116
Herdman, Jean Ellen, 139
homosexuality, 119, 148

Honey, Maureen, 18–20
Hopper, Hedda, 59–60, 94–95, 138–40, 149–51
horizon of expectations, 102
The House I Live In (1945), 74, 79–81, 82–83
Hurwitz, Beth, 109

Indianapolis Recorder, 73
Italian American identity, 75–81

James, Harry, 3, 34
Japanese Americans, 77–78, 79–81, 88–89
Jarman-Ivens, Freya, 113–14
Jarvis, Christina S., 35
Jauss, Robert, 102
Jenkins, Henry, 54
Jesse, Marianne, 69–70
journals of fan clubs, 52–55
juvenile delinquency, 30, 43–44, 46, 48–49, 78, 83–85

Kahn, E. J., Jr., 58–59, 88, 93–94, 113, 115–16
Keightley, Keir, 141, 143–44
Keppler, Victor, 92*f*
Kracauer, Siegfried, 147

Ladies' Home Journal, 26–27, 27*f*, 28*f*
lesbianism, 119–20
Los Angeles Times, 75, 129, 142, 149–50

Manzi, Lucille, 122–23
Marijane, 68–69
Martin, John, 121–22
masculinity representations, 31–40, 142–49
mass culture, 6–7
McCabe, Loretta, 106–7
McCloskey, Mark A., 45–48
McCracken's, Allison, 113–14
McNally, Karen, 148–49
McShane, Peggy, 117–18
media representations of masculinity, 31–40
Meet Danny Wilson (1952), 142–49, 145*f*, 146*f*
membership procedures of fan clubs, 55–58
Miller, Glen, 31–33
Miller, J. Howard, 18–20, 19*f*, 154
Miller, Neil, 119
Modern Screen Fan Club Association (MSFCA), 66–69, 104–5
Modern Screen magazine, 22–23, 59–61
Movie Stars Parade magazine, 65

nationalism, 89–100
Nelson Eddy Club, 69

Nelson Eddy Notes magazine, 69
Newman, Judith, 55–56
New Yorker, 58–59
New York Herald Times, 123–24
New York Times, 49, 86, 101–2
normative masculinity, 113–14
Nuzum, Richard, 73

Ora e Sempre Sinatra (Now and Always Sinatra) club, 57, 61–62, 85–86, 95
Our Guy Frankie Fan Club, 62–63, 70, 122

Palladino, Grace, 48–49, 135–36
Palmer, Jean, 111
Pearl Harbor bombing (1941), 15, 80–81
Photoplay magazine, 22–23, 69–70, 106–7
Piess, Kathy, 24–26
Pittsburgh Courier, 90–91
politics. *See* civil rights and politics
post-WWII culture
    introduction to, 13, 129–31
    Sinatra, Frank and, 137–41
    teenage girls and, 134–37
    women as working citizens, 131–34
premarital sex, 26–27, 30–31
Presley, Elvis, 5–6
propaganda, 16, 22, 31–32, 35, 45, 89–90, 91–92, 94, 97, 118–19
prostitution, 29–30, 138
purpose and professionalism of fan clubs, 51–71

racial discrimination, 12, 18–20, 49–50, 79–80, 88–89
Radio Mirror magazine, 22–23
Rat Pack, 4, 13–14, 153
Razlogova, Elena, 105–6
reader participation in fan magazines, 104–8
Reid, Helen, 56
religious discrimination, 12
resistors in fandom, 6–7
Riot Grrrl fandom, 5–6, 66, 103, 104–5
RKO Radio Pictures, 79, 82, 142
Rolling Stone magazine, 101–2
Roosevelt, Franklin D., 15, 75, 77–78, 85, 86–89
Roosevelt, Theodore, 63–64
Rosie the Riveter, 2, 13–14, 18–20, 19*f*, 22, 131–32, 154

Savage, Jon, 21
Scheuer, Philip K., 142
Schrum, Kelly, 26, 134–35

Screenland magazine, 22–23, 65, 107, 108*f*
segregation, 15–16, 18–20, 32, 48–50, 73, 79–80, 119
Semper Sinatra Fan Club, 68, 70, 94–95, 117, 120
Seventeen magazine, 134–36
Sinatra-ly Yours magazine, 68–69, 70, 85–86, 96, 117, 120
Sinatra Scope magazine, 109
The Sinatra Sender, 86
Sing with the Sinatras Club, 56, 62, 67–68, 82, 83, 97–98, 110, 116
Slaves of Sinatra club, 110–11
SPARs (Semper Paratus-Always Ready), 2, 17–18
Stanfill, Mel, 9–10
Stephens, Juanita, 62, 98
"The Sub-Deb" column in *Ladies' Home Journal*, 26–27, 27*f*, 28*f*
Swooner Crooner (1944), 1, 12, 38*f*, 38–40, 39*f*, 76–77, 99

teenage social organizations
    introduction to, 11–12, 41, 43–45
    journals of fan clubs, 52–55
    purpose and professionalism of fan clubs, 51–71
    Teen Canteens, 6, 11–12, 41, 44–51
Teen Canteens, 6, 11–12, 41, 44–51
teenyboppers, 5–6, 103
thumbnail sketches, 55–56
Time magazine, 40–41
T-Jacket Journal, 56, 62, 67, 82, 83, 98
tolerance, fan writings on, 81–89, 84*f*
Tsoule, Sophie, 123

Vallée, Rudy, 3, 5–6, 92–94, 113–14, 123–24
The Voice: The Story of an American Phenomenon (Kahn), 58–59, 88
The Voice journal, 70–71, 110, 125*f*
Voices Echo magazine, 62–63, 70
voting power of teens, 87

WAACs (Women's Army Auxiliary Corps), 2, 17–18
Warner Bros. Pictures, 1, 76
WASPs (Women Airforce Service Pilots), 2
WAVES (Women Accepted for Volunteer Emergency Service), 2, 17–18, 60
Weatherford, Doris, 17, 20
women's suffrage movement, 16–17
Woodward, Elizabeth, 26

World War II American culture. *See also* post-WWII culture
  introduction to, 1–2, 4–5, 15–16, 156
  media representations of masculinity, 31–40
  teen girl culture and, 21–31
  women's roles, 16–20

YANK: The Army Weekly magazine, 36
Yates, Dick, 120–21
YMCA, 45–46
Young at Heart (1954), 148–49
YWCA, 45–46